LEADER'S GUIDE

Dan and Joy Solomon
Creators

Debra Ball-Kilbourne
MaryJane Pierce Norton
Writers

Abingdon Press

FaithHome Leader's Guide

CIP data available from the Library of Congress.
ISBN 0-687-06600-X

This book is printed on recycled, acid-free paper.

97 98 99 00 01 02 03 04 05 06 — 10 9 8 7 6 5 4 3 2

MANUFACTURED IN THE UNITED STATES OF AMERICA

Contents

A Special Word to FaithHome Leaders

Many pastors and church leaders have feelings of frustration and guilt when it comes to helping parents "teach the faith" to their children. Where does one turn for help? How does one design a practical, productive approach?

Many church learning settings are not "family friendly." From family nights to Bible school, children and parents share in few experiences together.

Parents everywhere are voicing concern about their children's appropriation of the Christian faith. These same parents are often quite honest about their own feelings of inadequacy in knowing and teaching the faith.

Studies show that "home" is the most influential setting for faith development—more so than church or school or peer group. The good news is that many parents and children are prepared to make a serious, intentional commitment for their home to be a "faith home"!

FaithHome provides pastors, church leaders, parents, and children a focused, intentional, and enjoyable experience for faith formation. It is a

–road map for a faith journey;
–shared experience for children and parents (or caregivers);
–"learning through living" model of faith formation;
– holistic design that links major themes of the Christian faith with the natural unfolding of daily life;
–way for parents and children to share faith conversations comfortably.

FaithHome provides families who want a more faith-focused home a practical, positive experience for faith formation.

FaithHome enables congregations to provide a ministry for families as their faith home.

May God's Holy Spirit lead you as you lead others to be at home in the faith!

Dan and Joy Solomon

Introduction to FaithHome

Welcome to FaithHome, an exciting and fun experience in which families of all kinds come together to learn about God, the Christian faith, and how to be a "faith home"—a home in which talking about God and talking to God are a natural and comfortable part of everyday family life. Through the FaithHome experience, families also will discover that they are an important part of a larger "faith home," the church, where they both receive and give love, guidance, support, security, and encouragement as they seek to be faithful families in today's world.

As a FaithHome leader, you will guide families participating in the FaithHome experience in an exploration of basic beliefs about

- God
- Jesus
- the Holy Spirit
- the Church
  —as Learning Community
  —as Worshiping Community
  —as Witnessing and Serving Community
- Worship
- Living Sacramentally

The Apostles' Creed, one of the earliest affirmations of Christian belief, forms the backdrop against which each of these topics can be explored. As you spend time discussing these topics—so vital to developing faith—it is our hope that you will forge new bonds within your own family and with other Christian families who experience FaithHome with you.

HOW DOES FaithHome WORK?

Over the next nine weeks, you will lead a weekly session in the church building that focuses on each of the topics listed above. Just as family rituals are important in the home, so also are learning rituals. You will note that the weekly sessions in the church follow the same format, with some activities being repeated week by week. This repetition will enable both children and adults to try some new things and to make some new discoveries. The format for each session, which is planned for 75-90 minutes, includes the following:

—A brief welcome opens the session. (3 minutes)
—An energetic video segment, followed by brief discussion, introduces and connects the topic to the everyday lives of today's families. (10 minutes)
—An opening group activity involves everyone in an active exploration of the week's theme. (15 minutes)
—Separate sessions with adults and children speak to the needs and interests of each group. (40-45 minutes; **Note:** The children's session is broken up into various activities, keeping the children active and interested.)
—A closing activity involves the full group in reflection and worship. (15 minutes)

As you can see, FaithHome requires a minimum of two leaders for each session—one for leading the adult session and one—or more, depending upon the size of your group and the ages of the children—for leading the children's session. The two of you may decide to co-lead the opening and closing sessions, or you may choose to lead one session each.

In addition to video, music is an important part of each weekly session. An audiocassette is provided in the *Leader's Resources Kit*; additional cassettes may be purchased by individual families for home use if desired.

After the weekly group experience, participating families are to use the *Family Guide* for continued exploration and practice during the following week. In addition to a brief summary of the topic for the week, parents will find helpful suggestions and materials for the faith experience in the home, such as daily "Family Faith Breaks," which include Bible readings and sample prayers; "Talk Together" conversation starters; ideas and discussion guides for two special family meals each week; and a simple "Beyond the Family" outreach activity for each week, such as taking cookies to a neighbor who is ill.

Family meals are essential! Stress the importance of these times so that families are not tempted to skip them. Some of the things that might happen at a shared family meal include

- sharing family stories, including stories about extended family and parents' childhoods;
- a more relaxed, enjoyable meal;
- a time to "check things out" with other family members.

Many important decisions are made and many hurts are healed around the family table.

An optional retreat is included in this *Leader's Guide* to celebrate the FaithHome experience and the supportive relationships forged with other families. The retreat also encourages families to continue the new "rituals" or habits of shared family prayers, devotions, faith conversations, outreach activities, and special meals, including the use of the Christ candle, as they make a serious commitment to make their home a "faith home."

WHO CAN LEAD FaithHome?

FaithHome can be led by any two adults who want to help families develop a faith-focused home, whether they be laypersons, church staff members, pastors, or any combination of these.

There is much to be gained by the pastor being one of the FaithHome leaders. Children are genuinely affirmed when pastors take special notice of them. Parents are reassured when the pastor is one of their children's "teachers." Congregations are grateful that their pastor is clearly committed to children and the family. In addition, FaithHome affords every pastor the opportunity to "live and learn" with children, parents, and whole families. It is an "immersion experience" in the lives of families that equips every pastor for visionary leadership and relevant preaching.

If the pastor is not one of the FaithHome leaders, the pastor is encouraged to be present for some portion of each FaithHome session. This not only signifies the importance of the experience in the eyes of the church; it also demonstrates the pastor's concern for the faith formation of individual families and of the entire congregation. What's more, it is a wonderful opportunity for one-on-one interaction and relationship building! (See the *Pastor's Guide* for more information regarding the pastor's role in FaithHome.)

HOW DO I USE THE *LEADER'S GUIDE*?

The FaithHome *Leader's Guide* has been designed to be convenient and easy to use. Each week includes the following kinds of material:

 Wherever you see this icon, you will find background material related to the beliefs and ideas to be explored in each weekly session. Read the material thoroughly, even if it is familiar to you.

Then turn to the "Leader's Weekly Session Guide" and note the key points you are to present during the adult session. Now reread the background material, highlighting phrases and passages or making notes to use in the adult session. There is no "script" to be read; therefore you may tailor your presentation to fit your particular group. Keep in mind that you will have approximately 10 minutes to

introduce the key ideas. You may find it helpful to have the adults read the brief summary included in the *Family Guide* before each week's session. Remember: This material is not to be used for an in-depth study but for an introduction leading to discussion, inquiry, and continued learning.

 This icon appears periodically in the background reading material, indicating an exercise provided for your personal reflection. Doing these exercises will make you a more effective FaithHome leader by helping you internalize the material and giving you ideas and insights for relating to the adults in your group.

This icon flags the beginning of the "Leader's Weekly Session Guide." Here you will find the objectives for the FaithHome session at the church, a list of materials needed, and specific instructions for leading the session. Reproducible handouts, patterns, and other materials to be used in the session follow the session guide.

HOW DO I PREPARE TO LEAD FaithHome?

The following guidelines for preparation will increase your effectiveness as a leader:

- Acquaint yourself thoroughly with the materials in the *Leader's Resources Kit.*
- Before each session:
  —View the FaithHome video segment for that week.
  —Allow adequate time to review the material in this *Leader's Guide* and in the *Family Guide* and plan for the week's session.
  —Gather needed supplies (see materials needed for each session).
  —Reserve (if necessary) audiovisual equipment and audiocassette player and be sure that the equipment is in working condition.
  —Prepare a comfortable and inviting environment so that each participant can have a quality session.
- As much as possible, reduce unnecessary commitments during the nine weeks of the FaithHome experience so that you can offer quality leadership. You also might explore the possibility of releasing all participants from other church obligations during the experience (other than attending worship) to increase participation.
- Pray daily for each family as they participate in the experience. Likewise, invite other Christians to pray for you as you provide leadership.

- Remain open to the leadership of the Holy Spirit throughout the experience. God desires to do something new!
- Before beginning the FaithHome experience, it is essential that you hold a covenanting ceremony or service of commitment. The commitment is not only for the families and leaders taking part in the sessions; it is for the church as well. As the church, it is important that we demonstrate our support of this ministry. We need to let FaithHome participants know that we have taken them into our hearts and will pray for them and uphold them while they work together in strengthening their faith.

This outward show of support will encourage participation in the current sessions and create interest in future groups as well. Likewise, it is important to hold a closing ceremony at the end of the sessions. The whole church will wish to join in a service of celebration for the newly strengthened members. The *Pastor's Guide* contains more information on these services.

With these words of guidance, turn now to the following list of "Questions and Answers for FaithHome Leaders" to find other important information and details necessary for leading a FaithHome experience in your church.

QUESTIONS AND ANSWERS FOR FaithHome LEADERS

What time and setting are appropriate for FaithHome?

FaithHome is a nine-week experience to be held at the church at a time convenient for the participants, whether that be a Saturday morning, Sunday evening, or other night during the week. Because each session is planned for 75-90 minutes, FaithHome is not designed for the traditional Sunday school hour.

It is readily apparent that faith formation cannot be "accomplished" in nine weeks. However, this nine-week experience is an important first step that, when faithfully followed, begins to establish a pattern of possibilities for faith development. Recognizing that nine weeks is only a beginning, some FaithHome leaders and groups may want to be intentional about expanding the experience over a longer period of time.

The room or rooms you choose for your weekly gathering will depend upon the size and makeup of your group. If at all possible, it is recommended that you meet in a large Sunday school class, meeting room, or fellowship hall during the opening and closing times and have the children move into another room when it is time for the separate adult and children's sessions. If you choose to remain in the same room during this time, set up an area for the children's session in one corner or section of the room. Be sure to have all the equipment and materials in place and "ready to go" well in advance. *(Remember to have small tables and chairs for the younger children.)*

Can a meal be part of the weekly church experience?

Many churches have a meal together one night a week, which provides a natural setting for gathering interested families together. The weekly FaithHome sessions could follow such a meal. However, it is recommended that the FaithHome session take place in a room separate from the meal so that equipment and materials can be set up and ready for use.

Whether churches regularly host a weekly meal or do not, a time for eating together could be an effective part of the FaithHome experience. Each FaithHome group can make this decision according to their needs, or perhaps a group may want to experiment with different possibilities over successive FaithHome sessions. (Note: The 75-90 minutes planned for the weekly FaithHome experience does not include time for a meal. You will need to allow an additional 30-45 minutes for this.)

What families can participate in FaithHome?

FaithHome is designed for all families—whether they be two-parent families, single-parent families, blended families, foster homes, or any other kind of family. Grandparents, aunts, uncles, and other extended family members or primary caregivers are also welcome to sponsor children in the FaithHome experience. The only requirement is that every child who participates has at least one caregiver who commits to attend with him or her.

What ages of children can participate?

FaithHome has been developed primarily for families with children ages four to twelve. However, families who have children in this age range and who also have teens are encouraged to attend as a family. During the time when the adults and children break into separate groups, teens may choose to participate in the adult session or to assist with the children's session, acting as "helpers" or "mentors" for younger brothers and sisters. Likewise, families who have children in the recommended age range and who also have one or more children under age four are encouraged to participate. Each FaithHome group may decide whether to provide child care at the church for children under age four. (Note: Even if your group does not include children under age four, it is recommended that you consider having one or more additional youth or adult "helpers" present at each weekly gathering to assist with the younger children as necessary, particularly if you have a large number of younger children in your group.)

What is the purpose of the video segment for each group session?

Video is extremely important for an effective and successful FaithHome experience. Each weekly gathering begins with a fast-moving, upbeat video segment that will engage and focus the attention of both children and adults. It also will introduce them to the key themes of each session. Each video segment features real people of all ages responding to some important faith questions. The purpose of the video is not to attempt to present the "answers" to these faith questions. Rather, its purpose is simply to introduce the questions.

It is likely that some individuals in your group may disagree with some of the responses they hear, and that is perfectly acceptable. After playing the video segment, invite participants of all ages to share their thoughts about the questions and responses they have heard and encourage discussion among the group. You might try eliciting responses with questions such as

How would you respond to the question . . . *(repeat one of the questions from the video)*?
Which response did you like most? Why?
Which response did you like least? Why?
Which responses surprised you?
Which responses made you laugh?
Is there a particular response you expected to hear but did not?

Remember, the primary purpose of the video is to draw participants into the key themes of the week and prepare them to share their own thoughts and ideas.

What do I need to know about the separate session with the children?

The children's session is designed to be set up as three different activity centers, with a full-group circle time at the beginning and at the end of the session. This will keep the children active and interested as they move from one activity to another, spending no more than 10-15 minutes on any one activity.

How the children move through the centers will depend upon the makeup of your group. If you have a small group, a group of mostly older children, or three or more youth or adult "helpers" who can assist the children in the centers, let the children rotate through the centers in small groups after the opening circle activity. After dividing the children into groups, point out the activity in each center and explain what they are to do; or have a helper in each center to provide instructions and assistance.

If you have a large group and few helpers, or if your group consists of mostly younger children, do each of the three activities sequentially as a full group between the opening and closing circle times.

Each week be sure to read the instructions carefully, check the materials needed, and set up the activity centers well in advance of the session. Remember that you will need small tables and chairs for the younger children.

Will we be able to cover all the activities provided for the adult and children's sessions within the suggested time frame?

The weekly FaithHome experience is designed to last 75-90 minutes. Within this time frame, 40-45 minutes have been allotted for the separate sessions with adults and children. As explained previously, the children's session is broken into short segments involving a variety of activities to hold the children's attention and interest. To prevent your weekly FaithHome session from running over and to allow sufficient time for families to interact together, it is important not to exceed this 45-minute limit.

Time estimates are given for all the activities provided for both children and adults. Please note, however, that these are *estimates*; they will vary according to the makeup and dynamics of your particular group, including your own presentation style. Some weeks you may find it difficult to do everything that is suggested. Feel free to modify the activities as necessary to meet the needs of your group. Sometimes this may mean that you choose to do one activity rather than another. Or you may find ways to simplify or shorten a suggested activity. The important thing is to achieve the stated objectives for each week's FaithHome session. You can do this by carefully reviewing the leader's session guide and tailoring the material for your particular group in advance of the weekly gathering. Then, as the session progresses, make adjustments as necessary to keep things moving and stay "on schedule."

What is the Christ candle, and what is its purpose?

The lighted Christ candle represents Christ with us and reminds us that Jesus came to be the Light of the World. The Christ candle is an important symbol used during the closing time of each weekly FaithHome session as well as during family meals at home during the week. As leader, you will need one Christ candle for the weekly group sessions; each participating family will need their own Christ candle for use at home. For the final weekly FaithHome session, each family is to bring their Christ candle with them and light it from the one you have lighted. This is to signify our willingness to go forth in the name of Christ to witness and to serve.

Christ candles generally are large, white pillar candles. A Christ candle may be plain or may have symbols decorating its front. Two particularly appropriate symbols for FaithHome are the

Chi Rho (formed from the first two letters of the Greek word for Christ) or a symbol representing the Holy Trinity. Both plain and decorated Christ candles are readily available at most Christian bookstores. Plain white pillar candles also can be purchased at most variety stores.

What kinds of activities will participating families be doing at home each week?

The *Family Guide* provides background reading and specific ideas and activities to help families continue learning and growing in faith at home—including things to talk about together each day, daily family devotions with Scripture passages and Bible helps, plans for two special family meals each week, and a weekly activity for reaching beyond the family. Also provided in the *Family Guide* is a tear-out table tent card with the Apostles' Creed printed on one side and the Lord's Prayer printed on the other. Each family is to place the tent card on their family table, or in another prominent place, and practice saying and learning the creed and prayer together at mealtime, during "Family Faith Breaks," or at other times. Families also may want to purchase a FaithHome audiocassette tape for use at home during the week.

What happens after the nine-week FaithHome experience has ended?

The last week of FaithHome focuses on how families can become "faith homes" by continuing the habits they have been learning and practicing during the FaithHome experience. A final emphasis is given to prayer and sacramental living—recognizing God's presence in the ordinary routines, events, and people of daily life. The optional retreat included in this *Leader's Guide* is an effective culminating event during which participating families can celebrate their shared experience and make a commitment to continue the experience as individual families. Some families may choose to make a covenant to provide encouragement and support to one another in the weeks and months to come as they strive to become "faith homes." (See the *Pastor's Guide* for more information about expanding and enhancing the FaithHome experience.)

FaithHome Nine-Week Overview

As previously mentioned, FaithHome is loosely woven around the Apostles' Creed as the historic creedal statement of the Christian church. Parts of the beliefs stated in the Apostles' Creed are examined in each weekly session. The goal is that parents and caregivers will examine their own beliefs as children examine theirs and that, in talking with one another, all will grow in faith. As the FaithHome experience progresses, families create a banner that reflects the beliefs or topics they are exploring, adding a symbol to the banner each week. (Patterns for these symbols follow the "Leader's Weekly Session Guide" for each week.)

WEEK 1: Symbol: Crest

This session introduces the FaithHome experience, the Apostles' Creed, the value of affirmations of faith, the Lord's Prayer, and the importance of prayer to faith development and to the FaithHome experience. The session also explores, in a beginning way, what children and adults believe and how they can begin to make prayer a vital part of family life.

WEEK 2: Symbol: Heart

This session explores who God is and how we think and talk about God. It acknowledges that God is known by many names and explores more fully God the Father and God the Creator.

WEEK 3: Symbol: Cross

In this session, participants learn and talk about Jesus—both the Son of God and the man who lived and taught. The focus is on Jesus' life and how Jesus helps us know God.

WEEK 4: Symbol: Flame

This session focuses on the Holy Spirit: God with us. Because this concept is harder to define for children, examples are given of other things we experience and know to be true but cannot see.

WEEK 5: Symbol: Fish

This session explores how the church learns together—specifically, how we learn about Jesus and God and how we learn from one another. Special consideration is given to the roles of the church and the family in teaching the faith.

WEEK 6: Symbol: Butterfly

In this session, participants explore why and how we worship together as a church family. The focus is on the congregation as a community of faith, a "faith home." Special attention is given to rituals of worship—specifically to the sacraments of baptism and Holy Communion.

WEEK 7: Symbol: Candle

Families learn what we mean by Kingdom living as they explore how and why we, the church, witness and serve by sharing our faith in words and actions.

WEEK 8: Symbol: Bible

This session focuses on how we as individual families share the Bible together and how this sharing is essential to faith development in the home. In addition to discussing the importance of the Bible for Christians, families identify familiar Scripture passages and explore different translations of the Bible.

WEEK 9: Symbol: Praying Hands

Families revisit the topic of prayer and explore what it means to live as a "faith home" and how living sacramentally—experiencing and celebrating God's presence each and every day—is a part of that experience. The importance of family rituals is also explored.

I Believe . . .

An American couple on a mission trip to Russia walked down a dimly lit street in Moscow. A man approached them with the obvious intent of getting their attention. He said, "I know who you are." Then he took a small cross out of his pocket and cradled it in the open palm of his hand. "I, too, am a believer," he said. In those moments, believing forged a sense of bonding. Though they came from another country and another culture, the American couple understood something vitally important about who this man was and what he believed.

In one way or another we are all believers. We may believe, for example, that sugar promotes hyperactivity, that pets are helpful in teaching children responsibility, or that parents need time away from the demands of parenting. As Christian people, we have important convictions about God and the way God plans for us to live.

This first session of FaithHome seeks to

—explore what it means to believe;
—help families create their own symbols of belief;
—introduce persons to the Apostles' Creed and other creedal statements;
—help persons and families begin to formulate personal statements of belief;
—introduce persons to the Lord's Prayer and explore the importance of prayer to faith development.

 ## LEADER BACKGROUND MATERIAL

We Are All Believers

Attitudes and actions flow from our beliefs. Some years ago, one family experienced the practical realities of this fact when their youngest child unjustifiably provoked an encounter with a neighbor child. Swiftly disciplining him, the parents asked him why he had done such a thing. He answered, "Because I thought 'we' hated them." Pressed further, he explained that he had heard his parents commenting on how their neighbor—the child's father—constantly flicked cigarette stubs in his yard. The prevailing winds carried the stubs into their yard, creating a mess and upsetting the boy's family. The child, hearing his parents' comments, thought

they "hated those folks." Having come to belief, he was moved to action. Needless to say, his parents tried hard to change their son's belief, even as they dealt with their own shame about their comments.

The genocide of six million Jews and multitudes of those "unacceptable" to the Third Reich because of heritage, lifestyle, or political and religious viewpoints was essentially because of belief. More recently, ethnic cleansing in Bosnia evolved because persons believed others of differing ethnic or religious backgrounds were somehow of less intrinsic worth. For good or ill, what we believe affects our actions and attitudes.

Throughout the centuries, Christians have grappled with convictions about God. In the early years of Christianity, a carefully crafted statement set forth beliefs that helped to shape Christian identity and action. Known today as the Apostles' Creed, the statement describes major Christian beliefs that Christians can embody and live out in the world. These are the same beliefs that Christians have sought to embody and live out for two thousand years. They are the beliefs that were cherished and handed down across the generations, beginning with the earliest Christians. They are the essential beliefs for Christians to carry for themselves and to pass along to their children. For these reasons, we will focus on the beliefs outlined in the Apostles' Creed throughout FaithHome.

Various suggestions and materials are provided in this *Leader's Guide* as well as in the *Family Guide* to help families become more familiar with the creed and embrace the basic beliefs it affirms. One of these tools is a table tent card with the Apostles' Creed printed on one side and the Lord's Prayer printed on the other (see "Learning to Pray," page 18). Encourage each family in your FaithHome group to place the tent card on their family table, or another prominent place, and to practice learning and saying both the Apostles' Creed and the Lord's Prayer together throughout the FaithHome experience— during family meals and "Family Faith Breaks" or at other times.

The Apostles' Creed

The Latin word for "I believe" is *credo*, from which the English word *creed* derives. The root of the Latin *credo* is found in two words—*cor*, which means heart, and *dare*, which means to give or render. Thus, a creed or statement of belief is a declaration of how one thinks and how one intends to act. A creed is a statement of faith that takes its name from the word for *believe*.[1] The word *apostle* means "those sent on a mission." In the New Testament, Jesus—himself sent by God on a mission of salvation—sent out disciples to bear witness to the good news of God's transforming grace and power. Those sent out were called apostles.

The Apostles' Creed

**I believe in God the Father Almighty,
 maker of heaven and earth;**

**And in Jesus Christ his only Son our Lord:
 who was conceived by the Holy Spirit,
  born of the Virgin Mary,
  suffered under Pontius Pilate,
  was crucified, dead and buried;
 the third day he rose from the dead;
 he ascended into heaven,
  and sitteth at the right hand of God
  the Father Almighty;
 from thence he shall come to judge the
  quick and the dead.**

**I believe in the Holy Spirit,
 the holy catholic* church,
 the communion of saints,
 the forgiveness of sins,
 the resurrection of the body,
 and the life everlasting. Amen.**

*universal

"Fools say in their hearts, 'There is no God.' " So proclaims the first line of Psalm 53. Ancient words remind us that not all can say the powerful life-changing first words of the Apostles' Creed: "I believe in God the Father Almighty, maker of heaven and earth." At the time the Apostles' Creed was first proclaimed, however, many were anxious to affirm a newfound belief in one God. Monotheistic faith had been a belief of the Jews. New Christians, however, were often not Jews but Gentiles, some of whom had earlier embraced the pagan belief in the many gods of Canaanite, Roman, or Greek culture. The Apostles' Creed was an early attempt to bear witness that Christians believed in one true God, revealed first in Hebrew Scripture and fully revealed much later in the life, death, and resurrection of Jesus Christ.

Despite differences among Christian people, the statement "I believe in God the Father Almighty, maker of heaven and earth" serves as a common bond among believers. However differently the various streams of Christian faith may articulate the reality of God or live out their understanding of

God, the Apostles' Creed serves as a bridge—reminding Christians throughout the world that, despite the things that sometimes threaten to separate us, we have a rich, common heritage.

Scholars remind us that the apostles themselves did not compose the creed; they were dead long before the creed came into the written form we have today. They did, however, live out the message of the creed in joyful, faithful witness as followers of Jesus. Thus, the creed bears their name.

The content of the creed was closely related to its use in baptismal services, perhaps as early as the first century following Jesus' ministry. Candidates for baptism, brought before the congregation, were invited to declare their faith, much as we continue to proclaim the Christian faith today. However, for these early Christians, proclaiming the creed was more than simply reciting important information. To affirm the creed was to embark on a new way of living. In a sense, the Apostles' Creed became for newly baptized converts marching orders for a lifestyle of apostleship. During times of Christian persecution, proclaiming the creed might have been a literal life or death decision. So, while the present form of the Apostles' Creed can be traced back to the sixth century, its words, phrases, and usage reach all the way back to the earliest Christians.

In his book *Loyalty to God,*[2] Ted Jennings points out that the Apostles' Creed was meant to be a matter of the heart and, therefore, was not written down until several centuries of church life had unfolded. In fact, some leaders of the church warned against recording it, lest the creed become mere words and not a testimony to a particular character or quality of life resulting from a change in heart.

What About the Other Creeds?

Over the course of time, as the Christian church has grown and spread throughout the world, Christians have affirmed their faith through many different creeds. The Nicene Creed, prominent in Eastern Christianity, was completed in the year A.D. 381.

Christians today not only affirm their faith through ancient creeds but also make fresh statements about God, Jesus, and the Holy Spirit. Eduard Schweizer wrote, "The church must continue to make fresh statements about who Jesus is. It can never reduce these statements to a single final formula that would define Jesus for the rest of time."[3] So, in our own time, Christians affirm the Christian faith through "A Modern Affirmation." Christians of one nation use affirmations developed by believers in other nations or by Christians of other cultures, such as "A Statement of Faith of The Korean Methodist Church" and "A Statement of Faith of the United Church of Canada."

A Statement of Faith of the United Church of Canada

We are not alone, we live in God's world.
We believe in God:
    who has created and is creating,
    who has come in Jesus, the Word made
       flesh,
       to reconcile and make new,
    who works in us and others by the Spirit.
We trust in God.
We are called to be the church:
    to celebrate God's presence,
    to love and serve others,
    to seek justice and resist evil,
    to proclaim Jesus, crucified and risen,
       our judge and our hope.
In life, in death, in life beyond death,
    God is with us.
We are not alone.
Thanks be to God. Amen.*

*By permission of The United Church of Canada

Many congregations develop their own statements of faith, regularly interchanging the historic and recently developed creeds in worship, finding that each creed reflects deep devotion to eternal truths. The Apostles' Creed, however, retains its importance as perhaps the earliest creed of the Christian movement. Its brevity, comprehensiveness, and bold witness make it a creed for followers of every age.

Christians wanted to proclaim their faith in creedal form. Comparing the creeds can be a valuable exercise for Christians today. Even more valuable, however, is taking the opportunity to phrase our individual Christian beliefs.

    —What do you believe?
    —What can you affirm about the Christian faith?
    —Who is God to you? the Holy Spirit? Jesus Christ?
    —What is your relationship to other believers?
    —What is your purpose in life?
    —What does God intend for the world?

Before embarking on a journey of empowering others in their faith development, explore your own belief system. In the space provided, state what you believe.

Your statement is a beginning statement only, to be revised as you encounter new understandings throughout the FaithHome experience.

I believe . . .

Prayer: Essential to Faith Development

Perhaps nothing is more essential to faith development than prayer, which is why prayer is a predominant theme throughout the FaithHome experience. Prayer might be described as a way both to explore and to express our beliefs. Prayer is the way we communicate with God. How much easier it is to know someone intimately if we can communicate with him or her! Through prayer we talk with God about our beliefs, joys, desires, concerns, questions, and innermost thoughts. Prayer draws us closer to God. We would not be far off to call prayer the pipeline to the heart of God.

Simply put, prayer is conversation with God. But talking to God is not all we must do when we pray! When have you ever enjoyed a "conversation" with someone who did all the talking and did not listen to what you wanted to say? Good prayer is a two-way conversation. Prayer is not just a time for us to dump our concerns on God. To be sure, God wants us honestly and completely to share our innermost concerns and feelings in prayer. Look at how honest many of the psalms are in expressing emotions that we often would suppress. And yet prayer involves at least as much listening as talking. Sometimes we just have to be quiet so that we can hear what God has to say!

God Helps Us to Pray

If prayer is simply "conversation," we all should be experts, right? The truth is, many people find it difficult and uncomfortable to pray. One of the most miraculous aspects of prayer is that God helps us to pray when we do not know how to pray! Sometimes we do not know how to begin or what to say. Other times we draw a blank and cannot articulate what is on our hearts and minds. There also are times when we are so stunned or shocked by something that we are left speechless. Whatever the case may be, God's Holy Spirit takes our inarticulate yearnings and needs before God and actually prays on our behalf. God prays to God for us (see Romans 8:26-27)!

Consider this: If we have this promise from God that God will pray when we do not know how, then nothing and no one can prevent us from praying! Knowing this gives us the freedom and confidence to pray simply and honestly—without worrying about what words we use or how we sound. As Jesus told his disciples, "When you are praying, do not heap up empty phrases as the Gentiles do; for they think that they will be heard because of their many words. Do not be like them, for your Father knows what you need before you ask him" (Matthew 6:7-8).

Learning to Pray

Jesus assured his disciples that they need not worry about the words of their prayers because God already knew their needs; yet on one occasion, they asked him to teach them how to pray (see Luke 11:1). They had observed Jesus praying on his own, and they wanted to know how he prayed so that they could pray similarly. When they made this request, they were not in a synagogue or in the Temple. Likewise, we can learn how to pray outside of formal church settings. In fact, prayer probably is learned best in the home.

The Lord's Prayer, which Jesus used to teach his disciples how to pray, is a good starting point for most families. That is why the Lord's Prayer is printed on one side of the table tent card provided in every *Family Guide*. The idea is for every family participating in FaithHome to place the tent card on their family table, or in another prominent place, and to practice learning and saying the Lord's Prayer together—along with the Apostles' Creed— throughout the FaithHome experience—before family meals, during "Family Faith Breaks," or at other times.

In the Lord's Prayer, we are invited to approach God in the intimacy of a child's relationship to a parent. We are children of God! We are guided to come to God in awe of God's holiness and to pray for God's will on earth to be realized. We are confirmed in our need for daily sustenance for the body and for the nourishment of our souls. We are invited to depend upon God amidst temptation and evil in the confidence that what is true and eternal comes from God.

Another traditional approach to prayer that families may find helpful is the A-C-T-S model:

A: Adoration: Praising God is the essence of worship for both the family and the congregation. God is appropriately honored and glorified. Our inner being is attracted toward God. We want nothing more than to bask in God's presence and glory.

C: Confession: God invites us to "get honest"—a remarkable invitation. Our sin never outruns God's grace. Through prayers of confession, we discover, once again, how healing God's grace is. Prayers of confession confirm the reality of sin in our lives. More important, however, is the avenue it opens for a continuing and honest relationship with God.

T: Thanksgiving: We recognize the extent to which God has blessed us and how dependent we are upon God. So we say, "Thank you" to God.

> Blessed be the LORD,
>   for he has heard the sound of my
>   pleadings.
> The LORD is my strength and my shield;
>   in him my heart trusts;
> so I am helped, and my heart exults,
>   and with my song I give thanks.
>
> (Psalm 28:6-7)

S: Supplication: We petition God to supply something, either to ourselves or to someone else. Jesus himself offered prayers of intercession. Jesus said to Peter, "I have prayed for you that your own faith may not fail" (Luke 22:32). Prayers of intercession and petition seek unity between God's action and the actions of others, including our own actions.

Many parents wonder, "Are we to teach our children that their prayers can change God's mind and change the shape of events around us?" We may intuitively sense the danger in that possibility! On the one hand, disappointment can be the result when prayers are not answered—at least not in the way the petitioner had wanted. On the other hand, we know that prayer is not a magical incantation that forces God to do our will like a genie in a bottle.

Yet there is scriptural evidence that prayers have changed things, even God's mind. We should not presume to know whether or when or how this really happens. It is enough that we are told by Jesus and by others in the Bible that we are to offer our prayers—including prayers of supplication—to God.

Whatever method we use, we learn to pray by actually doing it. For the next nine weeks, families participating in FaithHome will learn more about prayer and how to pray together as a family. As they continue to "practice praying" together, as well as individually, they will become more and more comfortable and confident in the habit of prayer. It is our hope that by the end of the FaithHome experience, prayer will be a natural habit of daily family life, enabling families to become the "faith homes" that God is calling them to be!

◆ LEADER'S WEEKLY SESSION GUIDE

Week 1: I Believe

Objectives:

By the end of the session, adults and children will have
—explored what it means to believe;
—created a family symbol of belief;
—been introduced to the Apostles' Creed and other creedal statements;
—begun to formulate a personal statement of belief;
—recognized the importance of prayer to faith development and to the FaithHome experience;
—been introduced to the Lord's Prayer.

Materials Needed:

For Full Group: FaithHome video, video player and monitor, construction paper, scissors, glue, fabric glue, crayons and markers, crest patterns (see page 23), large piece of sturdy material for each family (approximately 1 yard x 1½ yards), Christ candle, matches, audio tape player, FaithHome tape

For Adults: copies of the Apostles' Creed (page 25), newsprint, markers, tape, writing paper, pencils or pens, *Family Guides*

For Children: copies of the Apostles' Creed (page 25), signing motions for the Apostles' Creed (page 24), ball, shoe box for each child, white paper, magazines or old curriculum, scissors, glue, crayons and markers, "Yes" and "No" signs (see page 21), construction paper, audio tape player, FaithHome tape, copies of the Lord's Prayer poster (page 26)

Welcome and Introduction (3 minutes)

Welcome the group and introduce yourself and any other FaithHome leaders, if necessary. Ask one member from each family to introduce his or her family group and to tell why they have chosen to be a part of FaithHome. Thank everyone for being present for this first session of FaithHome and briefly describe the purpose and objectives of the experience (see "A Special Word to FaithHome Leaders," page 5). (Note: This first welcome and introduction may take longer than 3 minutes, particularly if your group is large.)

Video Segment (10 minutes)

Tell the group that you will begin each weekly session with a short video segment, which will present the key themes for the week. Each video segment will feature real people of all ages responding to some important faith questions. The purpose of the video is *not* to attempt to present the "answers" to these faith questions. Rather, *its purpose is simply to introduce the questions*. In fact, individuals in your group may disagree with some of the responses they hear, and that is perfectly acceptable. After playing the video segment, invite participants of all ages to share their thoughts about the questions and responses they have heard and encourage discussion among the group. You might try eliciting responses with questions such as those listed on page 11. Conclude the discussion by asking these questions:

What forms of address or images did the people in the video use for God? What other images can we use to describe God?

Explain that God is portrayed through a variety of images throughout the Bible—including images such as nurturer (Psalm 23), judge (Genesis 18:25), father (Mark 14:36), mother (Isaiah 66:13), good shepherd (John 10:11), protector (Isaiah 46:3-4), midwife (Psalm 22:9-10), and others. The rich diversity of names we use to address and describe God will be an important topic of the second week, when we explore our belief in God as maker of heaven and earth.

Group Activity (15 minutes)

After viewing the video segment at every FaithHome session, each family will work together to create a symbol for a family banner, which they will take home with them at the end of their FaithHome experience. This week they will make family crests to place in the center of their banners.

On each table, place crest patterns (page 23), construction paper, scissors, crayons and markers, a large piece of material for each family (see materials needed), glue, and fabric glue. Instruct each family to cut a crest out of construction paper and then draw simple pictures and symbols or write words in each section of the crest to represent things that are important to them in the following four categories:

(1) What we enjoy doing together as a family
(2) What we spend the most time doing as a family
(3) What we believe as a family
(4) What we would like to do together but have a hard time doing

When each family is done, they may glue their crest to the center of a large piece of material.

Allow 15 minutes for the families to complete their work. Tell them that they will be sharing something about their crests during the closing time.

Adult Session (40-45 minutes)

(1) Repeat the questions from the video segment:

—What do you believe?
—What belief is most important?
—What does your church family give to you?

Allow for brief responses. Say something along these lines:

These questions get at the heart of what FaithHome is about. Our hope is that through these sessions at church and your conversations and activities at home during the coming weeks, you and your children will learn together, discuss together, and experience together what it means to be a "faith home"—a home where talking to God and talking about God and what we believe as Christians are a natural and comfortable part of everyday family life. (5 minutes)

(2) Hand out copies of the Apostles' Creed to each participant (page 25). Ask the group to read all the way through the creed and then to underline

statements they feel are particularly important to them. Ask individuals to share phrases or words or statements from the creed that they affirm. (Save these copies of the creed for use next week, if you like.) (5-7 minutes)

(3) Summarize the "Leader's Background Material" for Week 1, being sure to include the following points:

—The church through the ages has found it helpful to state what we believe.
—These statements are called "creeds."
—One of the oldest is the Apostles' Creed. (Include here some of the historical material included in the chapter.)
—Many other creeds have been written, and churches choose which ones they will use. (Highlight those commonly used in your congregation.)
—Prayer is two-way conversation with God.
—God's Holy Spirit prays on our behalf when we do not know how to pray.
—Prayer is essential to faith development and is best learned in the home. (Ask for some examples of "memorized" prayers that adults learned as children and still use. Talk about why these are powerful and need to be passed on to children.)
—The Lord's Prayer, which Jesus used to teach his disciples how to pray, is a good starting point for most families.

Briefly answer questions from the group. (10 minutes)

(4) Ask each person to reflect on the creedal statements you have read. Then have them reflect on their own beliefs and begin writing their individual statements of belief, responding to these questions (write the questions on newsprint):

(1) Who is God to you?
(2) Who is Jesus Christ to you?
(3) Who is the Holy Spirit to you?
(4) What is your relationship to other Christians?
(5) What is the purpose of the church?
(6) What is your purpose in life?
(7) What does God intend for the world?

Tell the participants that you are aware these are difficult questions; then instruct them to answer as briefly and quickly as possible, using single words or phrases. Emphasize that these do not need to be long, involved answers. This is a first attempt at thinking about what we actually believe and pass on to our children. Answer questions as they arise. Emphasize that these statements of belief need to be completed by each individual. Encourage each person to sign and date her or his statement. (8-10 minutes)

(5) Ask the group to stand and form an inner circle and an outer circle. Make sure each person is facing another person. Instruct them to talk directly to the person whom they are facing. Tell them you will be reading five statements. They are to complete each statement, then move as directed before completing the next statement. After giving each statement, ask the center circle to move two people counter clockwise while the outside circle stays in the same place.

> Statement #1: The easiest thing for me in stating my beliefs was . . .
> Statement #2: The most difficult thing in stating my beliefs was . . .
> Statement #3: As a parent, I am most confident in sharing my beliefs about . . .
> Statement #4: As a parent, I need the most help in sharing my beliefs about . . .
> Statement #5: As a parent, I feel prayer is important because . . . (4-5 minutes)

(6) Ask the group to sit. If you have not already distributed copies of the *Family Guide,* do so now. Explain what is expected at home during the week, emphasizing the family meals and the service opportunity that are provided for each week. Draw attention to the table tent card provided in each *Family Guide.* Printed on one side is the Apostles' Creed; on the other side is the Lord's Prayer. Tell the adults that they are to assemble and place the card on their family table—or another prominent place—and practice learning and saying the creed and the Lord's Prayer together as a family at mealtime and at other times. Young children can repeat each line or learn one phrase at a time. With regular repetition, many children will be able to recite all or part of both the Apostles' Creed and the Lord's Prayer by the end of the FaithHome experience. Answer questions from the group. (5-7 minutes)

Children's Session (40-45 minutes)

Note: *See page 11 for instructions regarding how to set up and lead the children's session.*

Opening Circle (5 minutes)

Invite the children to sit with you in a circle. Briefly play a name game. Toss the ball to each child in the circle. When a child catches the ball, ask the child to say his or her name and one thing he or she likes doing. Then ask the child to toss the ball back to you; repeat the child's name. Quickly move around the circle hearing and repeating the name of each child.

Ask the children:

What did you think about the video we watched?

Take *a few* statements from the group. Add statements of your own to help the children reflect on what they saw.

Show the children the activities that they will be doing.

Activity One: Art Center (10-15 minutes)

Me Boxes

Give the following instructions to the children:

Each of you choose a shoe box; then glue white paper to the top of the box. Write on the top of the box "My family." Then draw or cut and paste pictures from magazines that say something about your family.

For Younger Children: Glue the white paper to the shoe boxes for the children in advance. Assign an older child to help each younger child. Let the younger children color or draw what they wish on each side (rather than cut and paste).

Activity Two: Discovery Center (5 minutes)

"Yes/No" Game

This is a movement game. Post on one end of a table a sheet of paper with the word "YES" written on it. Post on the other end of the table a sheet of paper with the word "NO" written on it. Instruct the children to decide if they would say yes or no to each statement you read. When they decide yes or no, they move to the appropriate end of the table.

Use these statements:

(1) *Church is a place where we learn arithmetic.*
(2) *My parents are easy to talk to about God.*
(3) *Jesus was a man who loved children.*
(4) *It always snows in the summer.*
(5) *I like praying to God.*

(6) *Coming to church makes me glad.*
(7) *I can't see God, but I know God cares for me.*

Explain that how we answer these questions shows something we believe. Use these questions and the children's responses in the closing circle time.

Activity Three: Study Center (10 minutes)

For All Children: Read the Apostles' Creed aloud and explain that these words tell us what we believe as Christians. Tell the children that they will be learning about what these words mean and what we believe over the next several weeks. Invite volunteers to complete each of these statements:

> **I believe God is like . . .**
> **I believe Jesus is like . . .**
> **I believe the church is like . . .**

Now give each child a copy of the Lord's Prayer (page 26). After reading the prayer aloud, explain that this is the prayer Jesus used to teach his disciples to pray and that we, too, learn to pray as we learn the Lord's Prayer. Tell the children that prayer is an important part of FaithHome and that they will be praying with their families at home each day during the FaithHome experience. Give them a goal to strive for by suggesting that by the end of the nine weeks, they may be able to recite both the Lord's Prayer and the Apostles' Creed! If time allows, let the children color the Lord's Prayer to make posters for their rooms; or have the children color their posters at home during the week.

Closing Circle (10 minutes)

Call the children together in a circle. Let each child share one thing he or she has learned or done.

Using the poster on page 24, lead the children in signing the Apostles' Creed. Concentrate on the motions as you say the words. Encourage those who can read to say the words along with you. Remember, children often learn one skill at a time; do not worry if they cannot match the words with the motions. Let the children follow with their hands as you say the words. Tell the children they will be helping to lead the adults in these signs in a few minutes.

Briefly talk together about some of the things the children said they believe about God, Jesus, and the church. Tell the children they will be talking more each week about God, Jesus, and the church. End with a simple prayer of thanks for this learning time together.

Closing Time (15 minutes)

(1) As the children and adults come together, ask the adults to go with their children back to the tables where they worked on their crests. Invite each family to share one symbol from their crests that represents something about themselves as a family.

(2) After every family has had a chance to speak, ask the group to enter with you into a brief time of prayer. Light the Christ candle; then dim the lights. Pray, asking for God's guidance for each family present and for strength to enter into the commitment of study, discussion, reflection, and service. (After the prayer, turn the lights back on.)

(3) Say together the Apostles' Creed, letting the children lead with the motions they learned. (Of course, they will need someone to serve as leader, providing help and direction.)

(4) End with the songs "In Our Home" and "We Are Faith Families" (page 117), singing along with the FaithHome tape.

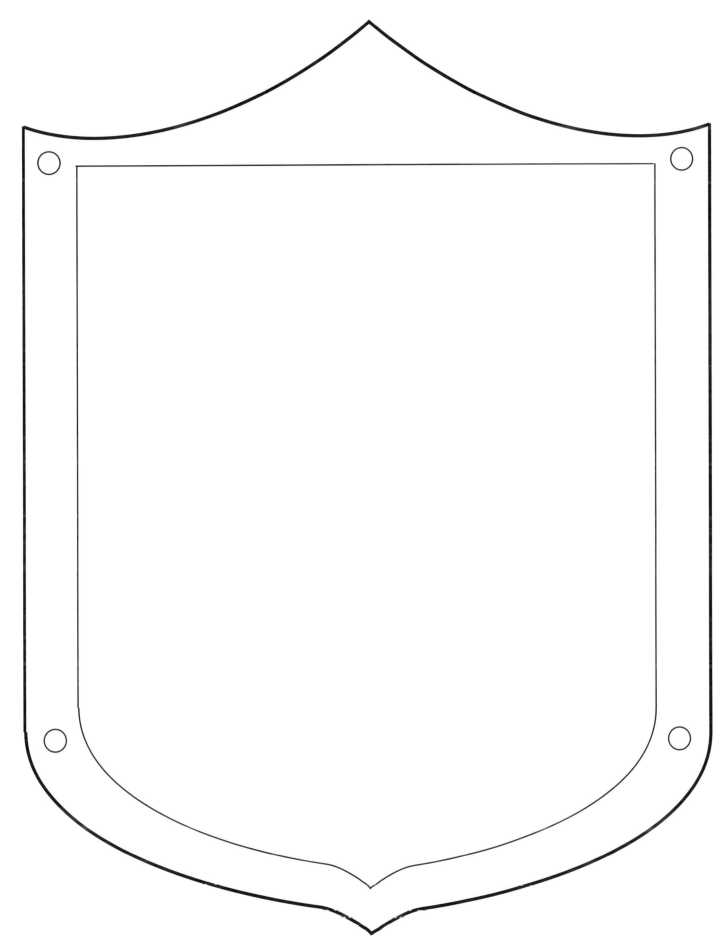

SIGNING MOTIONS TO THE APOSTLES' CREED

I believe in God the Father Almighty.

God

I believe in Jesus Christ his only Son our Lord.

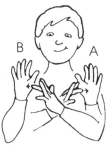

Jesus Christ

I believe in the Holy Spirit.

Holy Spirit

forgiveness

I believe in the forgiveness of sins.

I believe in the communion of saints, our church.

church

And I believe in the life everlasting.

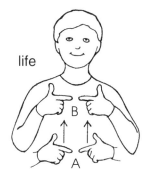

life

everlasting

Amen.

The Apostles' Creed

I believe in God the Father Almighty,
    maker of heaven and earth;

And in Jesus Christ his only Son our Lord:
    who was conceived by the Holy Spirit,
        born of the Virgin Mary,
        suffered under Pontius Pilate,
        was crucified, dead, and buried;
    the third day he rose from the dead;
    he ascended into heaven,
        and sitteth at the right hand of
        God the Father Almighty;
    from thence he shall come to judge
        the quick and the dead.

I believe in the Holy Spirit,
    the holy catholic* church,
    the communion of saints,
    the forgiveness of sins,
    the resurrection of the body,
    and the life everlasting. Amen.

*universal

The Lord's Prayer

**Our Father, who art in heaven,
hallowed be thy name.
Thy kingdom come,
thy will be done on earth as
it is in heaven.
Give us this day our daily bread.
And forgive us our trespasses,
as we forgive those who
trespass against us.
And lead us not into
temptation,
but deliver us from evil.
For thine is the kingdom, and
the power, and the glory,
forever. Amen.**

I Believe in God

"Why can't I see God?" the five-year-old child asked. How in the world should a parent answer that question and so many other questions equally as difficult?

Children want to know about God. They are intrigued by God. But they also are intrigued by Power Rangers, Ninja Turtles, and dozens of other amazing characters they watch every day through the "miracle" of television. Parents need help in assisting their children to distinguish between the marvelous realities of God, whom they cannot see, and the marvelous fictions of the action heroes they see every day. Parents need help in explaining the puzzles children wonder about concerning God, even when those parents have their own puzzles about God.

This week we will look at the reality of God as we know God through the power of creation. God is the One who created heaven and earth—all there is.

 ## LEADER BACKGROUND MATERIAL

Who Made God?

"Who made God?" is another question parents are sometimes asked. Awesome and timeless, the question is asked by each generation of believers. The answer is likewise timeless. God is eternal, not bound by time or space. Like a circle, God has no beginning. God was not made. God *is!* Only God can finally answer the question, "Who made God?"

Who made hope? Who made trust? We can identify reasons to hope. We can describe trustworthy people or trust-producing actions. Yet we cannot discover who made hope or trust. Hope and trust are spiritual realities that cannot be measured, charted, or analyzed by use of instruments. Yet, often we make life-changing decisions based on them. We may not know how either originated, but we give ourselves over to hope and trust again and again.

Small children often teach big lessons in trust. A five-year-old child shouts, "Catch me!" just before he or she jumps off the doghouse or launches from the side of the swimming pool. There is no calculation on the child's part that someone will not catch him or her. There is little doubt whether trustworthy

caregivers are adequate to the task. The question for the small child is, "Can I do it?" not, "Will they be there?"

Christians believe that God can be hoped in and trusted. In short, the One who was not created but is the Creator, who is not bound by time or space, can be counted on to "be there." Christians echo the thoughts of a hymn writer:

> **We believe in one true God,**
> **Father, Son and Holy Ghost,**
> **everpresent help in need,**
> **praised by all the heavenly host;**
> **by whose mighty power alone**
> **all is made and wrought and**
> **done.**[1]

In the Beginning   · · · use a story "Partners"

A couple waiting to adopt a child stood in the office of a social worker. Just moments before, they were childless. After twelve years of marriage, seemingly endless attempts to become pregnant, reams of paper work during an application process, and several routine home visits by case workers, a miracle was about to happen.

Husband and wife stood, holding hands, tentatively looking at the door. Opening it just a crack, a young woman holding a tiny infant entered the room. With tears streaming down her face, the birth mother placed the child in the arms of the adoptive mother. They had never met before; neither knew the other's name. Yet there was an intimacy unlike any other intimacy either had ever known. Together, they shared in the development of a child.

"Here he is," said the birth mother. "I have done everything I can for him. I love him. I cannot believe how much I love him. But now I give him to you. Raise him well. Help him to become the strong man I want him to be. Love him as your own."

Wiping a few tears with the back of her hand, the birth mother looked at her son in the arms of another woman. The room was strangely quiet, broken by only a few hushed tones of greeting as new parents welcomed their baby. It was a moment long to be remembered by everyone involved—a social worker, a birth mother, an adoptive couple, an infant son strangely oblivious to it all, and God. Throughout the long wait, certainly at its conclusion, there had been little doubt. God was "there," in some way addressing hurt and pain, nurturing hope and life. By the creation of new possibilities, by the salvaging of good from difficulties and troubles, God was "there," as God had been from the very beginnings of the world's creation.

In the Creation story we read,

So God created humankind in his image,
in the image of God he created them;
male and female he created them.

(Genesis 1:27)

Later, in Chapter 2, we read, "Then the LORD God formed man from the dust of the ground, and breathed into his nostrils the breath of life; and the man became a living being" (v. 7). These verses not only tell us that God "has always been," they also give us some very important insights into the nature of God. God created us; God is love. God breathed life into us; God is spirit. We are God's children, and God loves us.

God Is Love

Jesus' parable of the prodigal son is a story about a loving father who forgives a wayward son (see Luke 15:11-32). This parable also can be called "the parable of the loving father." The father not only forgives his son and welcomes him home, but he also throws a party for him, giving him the finest clothes to wear and the best food to eat.

Like the father in Jesus' parable, God is our loving Father, whose love is greater than we may ever be able to express or experience. Despite our rebellion, our sin, God forgives us and sees us as whole—as worthy of being children of God—with justice and mercy. God wants to heal, save, cleanse, help, forgive, guide, and encourage each of us as a child of God in faithful, fulfilled living.

Recall a moment of nurturing from your childhood. Or, if that is too difficult, recall a moment of nurturing you provided for another person.

—Was God a part of that moment?
—If so, can you describe how?

Honored by Many Names

Throughout the pages of Scripture, God is portrayed by means of a variety of images. Among those biblical images, God is presented as nurturer (Psalm 23); judge (Genesis 18:25); father (Mark 14:36); mother (Isaiah 66:13); good shepherd (John 10:11); protector (Isaiah 46:3-4); midwife (Psalm 22:9-10); and woman looking for a lost coin (Luke 15).

Many Christians find that one image alone does not adequately portray all that we experience about and from God. The writers of Scripture, for example, found it helpful to speak about God in a multitude of ways. The writers of our creeds, ancient and modern, and writers of theological treatises similarly use a variety of images to portray the richness of God's relationship with human beings.

Understanding God through a myriad of images is certainly nothing new to Christians! In the thirteenth century, Mechtild of Magdeburg in Germany prayed using a host of titles for God:

O burning Mountain, O chosen Sun,
O perfect Moon, O fathomless Well,
O unattainable Height, O Clearness
   beyond measure,
O Wisdom without end, O Mercy without
   limit,
O Strength beyond resistance, O Crown
   beyond all majesty:
The humblest thing you created sings your
   praise.[2]

Much earlier, in the fourth century after Christ, Saint Gregory declared, "No one who has given thought to the way we talk about God can adequately grasp the terms pertaining to God. 'Mother,' for example, is mentioned (in the Song of Songs 3:11) instead of 'father.' Both terms mean the same because there is neither male or female in God."[3]

Saint Cyril of Jerusalem, also writing in the fourth century, stated, "This alone will be a sufficient incentive to piety, to know that we have a God, a God who is One, a God who is, who is eternal, who is ever the self-same . . . who is honored under many names."[4]

God is "honored under many names" in the pages of Scripture, in the creeds of the Christian church, and in the hearts of believers.

—Under what names—through which images—do
   you describe God?
—How do you describe your relationship to God?
—Can the richness of your experience be
   summed up in a single image?
—Are many images required?

God the Father

Regardless of our affirmation of the richness of images through which God has been revealed, traditionally God has often been presented predominantly through male imagery. The Apostles' and Nicene creeds, for example, speak openly of God as Father. When so many other images of God can be found in the pages of Scripture, why would the developers of the creeds choose to describe God primarily by one title: Father?

Perhaps one reason is that Jesus often expressed his own relationship with God through the intimate title *abba*. Literally translated, *abba* means "Daddy." Jesus referred to God as Father many times in the Scriptures. In the Gospel of John, he uses this image 101 times. In the Gospel of Mark, he refers to God as Father four times. Some scholars note the fact that Mark's Gospel was probably the first written Gospel; therefore, the more minimal usage of *abba* is possibly significant. Later books, such as John, portray Jesus as favoring the image of God as Father far more often. Could it be that later Gospels reflect more of the early church's preference for this title rather than indicating a clear preference on the part of Jesus? Regardless, the image of God as Father clearly had great meaning for Jesus.

Jesus used other images for God as well. In his parables, Jesus portrayed God as a seeker of the lost—as a woman seeking a lost coin and as a shepherd hunting a lost sheep. He portrayed God as a baker, kneading dough, as well as a generous (and greatly begrudged!) employer. Can the multitude of images Jesus used help us in our understanding of God? Stated a bit differently, can predominant usage of one title for God distort the very nature of God within our understanding?

Tilden Edwards, writing in *Spiritual Friend*, may be quite correct when he advises, "Even though one dimension may have more value at a given point, the others are correct and fill out the image. One alone can become distorting and destructive."[5]

The very nature of God is to want to be known by all that God has created. Ironically, however, because we are human and therefore limited, we can never fully grasp the fullness of God. Our imperfect human language is incapable of comprehensively describing God. Once humans say everything we can say about God, mystery remains.

God the Creator

Christians believe that God is the Creator. Out of nothing—formless void—God created everything, according to Genesis 1:2. While there are wonderful "creations" that emerge from the fertile imaginations or determined spirits of human beings and while there are evolving forms of life all around us, these all build on God's previous act of Creation. The creating initiative of God is required for there to be meaning, beauty, order, fulfillment, completeness, and wholeness.

The first chapter of Genesis leads into the biblical witness with these words: "In the beginning God created the heavens and the earth." That single belief, affirmed so easily and authoritatively, serves as a foundation for everything else we believe about God. Shirley C. Guthrie, Jr., in his book *Christian Doctrine*, challenges us to see that "in the beginning" refers less to time measurement and more to reflecting belief about all new beginnings. In other words, God is the beginning Source and Power of creative initiative. "We and our world owe our existence to the constant flow of the creative and sustaining energy of God."[6] Even our own personal beginning reflects God's continuing creation. As the psalmist declared,

**For it was you [God] who formed my
  inward parts;
you knit me together in my mother's
  womb.**

(Psalm 139:13)

During the FaithHome experience, we are using one of the ancient creeds of the church, the Apostles' Creed, to reflect on our faith and to affirm it. The Apostles' Creed reminds us that "we believe in God the Father Almighty, maker of heaven and earth." The words of this creed, like many others, remind us that we believe in the One who has dominion over all of life.

To people of faith, there often is both great comfort and great meaning to be found in acknowledging that there is a God who has dominion and, therefore, One from whom we can ask guidance. We need not "go it alone," facing every temptation or trial as if it were "us against the world." We have the ability to seek guidance from One who is all-powerful and all-caring.

. . . It Was Good

The creation God has made—including the creation of human beings in God's own image—is good! Human beings were fashioned to show the image of the goodness of God and to share in a godly relationship with the Creator. Tennyson, in

Idylls of the King, wrote, "For good ye are and bad, but all like coins. Some true, some light, but everyone stamped with the image of the King." Because God made us, we are marked as good. Whether we bear witness to that goodness, of course, depends upon us.

Anne Frank wrote in her diary during the dark days of Nazi persecution, "Down deep inside I still believe people are basically good." Even as a teenager, she grasped a fundamental truth about God's creation. It is good! The qualities of being human are good! The fact that such qualities can be, and often are, used for evil does not nullify their basic goodness.

Creation is good because God made it good. Yet creation is not intended to be worshiped as God is worshiped. As Adam and Eve learned in the garden of Eden, creatures can never take the place of the Creator. We can and should praise God for creation. Yet to worship creation denies that God is the Ultimate Reality and robs God of our highest loyalty.

To say that God is Creator is to acknowledge that we are dependent upon God. To be dependent does not mean to be helpless before God. Good parents want to help children grow and develop. Given care, most children learn to do more for themselves and to express themselves openly. Even so, a child's survival in his or her young years largely depends upon others. Similarly, Christians believe that the survival of love, hope, forgiveness, reconciliation, and fulfillment requires that our lives be dependent upon God.

Nonetheless, God has made us the overseers of all creation (Genesis 1:26, 28); and God expects us to be wise stewards of it, respecting and using responsibly all that God has created.

In Week 7 we will explore these themes further as we focus on the church as a witnessing and serving community.

The Question of "How"

How did God make heaven and earth? That question really is not so important to ask and answer once we have settled for ourselves that we believe that God in fact made heaven and earth. However, many persons today worry and even argue about what are the appropriate roles of science and religion in considering the origins and creation of the universe and humanity.

It is important to note that science and the Bible are no more in opposition to each other than are apples and oranges. Scripture does not attempt to answer the question of "how" the universe was created. That is one of the concerns of science. To look for the "how" in the Bible is as foolish as attempting to get apple juice from oranges.

The Bible addresses the questions of "who" and "why." God is the Who. God is the Creator. The language Scripture uses to describe creation is "faith language." It is absolutely true. It is also absolutely not scientific!

If a man and a woman, in love with each other, agreed that their love surpassed the number of stars in the sky, they would be affirming a truth about their relationship. They would not be saying that if they counted the stars in the sky, they would have a way to measure precisely the extent of their love for each other. "Love language" is not meant to be scientific language. There is truth by which people live every day, even basing life-risking decisions on it, that is not scientific or verifiable truth. "In him we live and move and have our being" (Acts 17:28), proclaims the Bible.

Science has a variety of theories as to how the heavens and the earth came to be. Such theories can be welcomed for whatever insights they bring us for wholesome, fulfilled living in the world. However, science cannot prove or disprove God or the creative action of God or the transforming Spirit of God amidst creation. Christians believe that God created the heavens and the earth. God is still creating the heavens and the earth in a manner expressive of the very nature of God. What God creates is good!

We have explored how God is known through a variety of images, each of which is based in the pages of Scripture and in the faith statements of the church. As a Christian—and as a FaithHome leader—you may value some images more than others, based on how God has been revealed to you. Participants in your FaithHome group may have experienced God in meaningful but perhaps different ways.

Refer again to your personal creed you recorded on page 17 of this guide.

—What changes, if any, might you make in that personal creed based on your readings and reflections to this point?
—What do you reaffirm?
—Who is God?
—What is your relationship to God the Creator?

—What is the relationship of God to all human beings?
—Is creation good?
—Do humans have a responsibility within creation?

Write notes in the space below:

 LEADER'S WEEKLY SESSION GUIDE

Week 2: I Believe in God

use QV phrase God

Objectives:

By the end of the session, children and adults will have

- -talked about some of the words they use for talking to God;
- -stated questions and beliefs about God;
- -worshiped God together.

✂ Materials Needed:

For Full Group: FaithHome video, video player and monitor, family banners, construction paper, scissors, markers, heart patterns (page 35), glue, fabric glue, instant-developing camera and film, Christ candle, matches, audio tape player, FaithHome tape

For Adults: copies of the Apostles' Creed (page 25, or use copies from last week), newsprint, markers, tape, writing paper, pencils or pens, *Family Guides*

For Children: signing motions for the Apostles' Creed (page 24), copies of the "Talent Checklist" (page 36), heart patterns (page 35), construction paper, markers or crayons, stickers (see Activity 1), electric fan and facial tissue (see Activity 2), pencils, writing paper, Bibles, audio tape player and cassette tape (see Activity 3), FaithHome tape, copies of "Creation Word Search" (page 37), copies of "Match the Pictures" (page 38)

Welcome (3 minutes)

Welcome the group and thank them for being present for the second session of FaithHome. Ask them to introduce themselves again, if necessary, and share one thing they enjoyed from their "Family Faith Breaks" or "Family Meals" during the past week.

Video Segment (10 minutes)

Introduce the video segment by saying something like this:

This week we will be talking about God. Let's see what our friends on the video have to say. As you watch, think about how you would answer the questions. We will talk about that briefly after viewing the segment.

After playing the video segment, allow a few minutes for discussion (see page 11 for a list of questions to encourage discussion).

Group Activity (15 minutes)

This week each family will create a heart that shows who they are as a family who believes in God. On each table, place family banners, construction paper, heart patterns (page 35), markers, scissors, glue, and fabric glue. First, take pictures of each family using an instant-developing camera. Have each family cut a heart out of construction paper and glue their family's picture on it. Then tell them to draw small symbols or pictures and write words around the heart to show that they believe in God and that their belief in God is important to them. Then they may glue the heart to their family banner. Allow 15 minutes for the families to work together. Tell them that during the closing time they will be sharing something about the hearts they have made.

Adult Session (40-45 minutes)

(1) Repeat the questions from the video segment and allow the adults briefly to share their ideas.

—What is God like?
—What was your earliest image of God?
—And now?
—When do you feel closest to God?
—If you could ask God one question, what would it be?

OR

Invite the adults to talk about their experiences at home during the previous week. (5 minutes)

(2) Hand out copies of the Apostles' Creed (page 25). (Use the same copies from last week, if you like.) Ask the group to read all the way through the creed and then reread the statement about God in the first sentence. Have each person write the word "God" on his or her copy of the creed. Under "God," ask participants to write the phrases or words they think of first when they hear the word *God*. After a brief time, ask for volunteers to state some of the phrases or words they wrote down about God. If your group is small, you can go around the room and ask each person to share one word or phrase. Tell the group they can say what someone else has said if this is the word or phrase that has the most meaning for them. Record the responses on newsprint. Say something like this:

We'll probably hear some of these words or phrases again as we look at today's material. (8 minutes)

(3) Now have the adults think of some of the common questions their children have asked about God. Ask them to share some of these as you list them on newsprint. Tell the group you will come back to these later. (5 minutes)

(4) Summarize the "Leader's Background Material" for Week 2, being sure to include the following points:

—God is eternal, not bound by time or space.
—God is spirit. (Use the quote from Genesis 2:7: "Then the LORD God formed man from the dust of the ground, and breathed into his nostrils the breath of life; and man became a living being.")
—God is love. Tell the story of the prodigal son. Say:

This parable can also be called "the parable of the loving father."

—God's love is greater than we may ever be able to express or experience. God sees us as whole—as worthy of being a child of God—with justice and mercy.
—God wants to heal, save, cleanse, help, forgive, guide, and encourage each of us as a child of God in faithful, fulfilled living.
—We often see God best in terms of a parent who cares for us in the best way possible. Ideally, parents take care of every need of a child—for food, shelter, clothing, care, interest, love, responsiveness, consistency, and discipline for living successfully.
—Through the ages Christians have used a variety of images to portray the richness of God's relationship with us. Through the Bible, the tradition of the church, our own experiences, and others, we continually add to the ways we think about God and the names we use for God.
—Traditionally, Christians often have understood and addressed God as Father. Jesus often expressed his own relationship with God through the intimate title *abba*, meaning "Daddy."
—God brought us and every known thing into being; God has dominion over all of life. What God made is good. (10 minutes)

(5) Invite questions and responses from the group. When answering, try to move the group to reflection on what they think and feel their children's questions about the nature of God will be. (8 minutes)

(6) Instruct each person to find a partner. (Encourage couples to find different partners.) Assign each pair one question from the previously recorded list of children's questions (see #3). Let them decide together what an appropriate response to this question might be. After a brief time, listen to all the responses as a group. (8 minutes)

Children's Session (40-45 minutes)

Opening Circle (5 minutes)

Invite the children to sit with you in a circle. Briefly play a name game. Going around the circle, ask each child to stand and say, "My name is _____. I am a child of God, and I like to _____."

Ask the children:

What did you think about the video we watched?

Take a few statements from the group. Add statements of your own to help the children reflect on what they saw.

Show the children the activities that they will be doing.

Activity One: Art Center (10 minutes)

God Is Love Hearts

For Older Children: Give each child a copy of the heart on page 35. Ask the children to write on their papers "God is love" and then draw pictures inside the heart of ways they know God loves them. Some examples to give are food to eat, family, beautiful things they see in the world, and praying to God.

For Younger Children: Write "God is love" on each child's paper. Provide stickers such as praying hands, butterflies, animals, families, or others you can find. Let the children choose stickers to place on their hearts.

Activity Two: Discovery Center (5-10 minutes)

Talent Checklist

For Older Children: Hand each child a copy of the "Talent Checklist" (page 36.) Invite each child to circle those words that describe him or her. When they have finished, instruct each child to find another person, read her or his list, and then move to another person and do the same thing. When they have had a chance to review several lists, play a game. See who can remember the most about each person's list!

For Younger Children: Pair nonreaders with readers. Instruct the older children to read the words to the younger children and let them circle those that describe them. When exchanging lists, remain in younger child/older child pairs and have the older children read their lists to the younger children.

OR

Learn About God

Gather a small electric fan, facial tissue, crayons and markers, and paper. Turn the fan on to a low setting and say something like this:

Sometimes it's hard to believe in God because we can't see God with our eyes like we see other people. But there are other things we can't see, too. We can't see the wind, but we can see what the wind does. We're going to do an experiment. Each of you take a tissue. Hold it up in front of the fan. Watch what happens to it. Draw a picture or write what happens to things in the wind.

Invite the children to experiment with their tissues in front of the fan before writing or drawing pictures of "things in the wind."

Activity Three: Study Center (10 minutes)

For Older Children: Distribute Bibles and ask the children to turn in the Bibles to Genesis, Chapter 1. Have the children take turns reading Genesis 1:1–2:3. Then hand each child a copy of the "Creation Word Search" (page 37). Let them complete the activity, helping one another with the answers.

For Younger Children: Prepare a recording of Genesis 1:1– 2:3 in advance. Play the recording of the Creation story for the children. After listening to the tape, distribute copies of the "Match the Pictures" activity (page 38). Let the children match the pictures, assisting those who need help.

Closing Circle (10 minutes)

Call the children together in a circle. Let each child share one thing he or she has learned or done. Using the poster on page 24, lead the children in signing the Apostles' Creed. Concentrate on the motions as you say the words. Encourage those who can read to say the words along with you. Remember, children often learn one skill at a time; do not worry if they cannot match the words with the motions. Let the children follow with their hands as you say the words. Tell the children they will be helping to lead the adults in these signs in a few minutes.

Talk together about some of the things the children are learning about God. Listen to "Praise God, from Whom All Blessings Flow" on the

FaithHome tape and then sing along. End with a brief prayer of thanks for this learning time together.

Closing Time (15 minutes)

(1) As the children and adults come together, ask the adults to go with their children back to the tables where they worked on their hearts. Invite each family to share one thing from their heart that tells what they believe about God.

(2) After every family has had a chance to speak, ask the group to enter with you into a brief time of prayer. Light the Christ candle; then dim the lights. Pray, asking for God's guidance for each family present and for strength to continue the commitment of study, discussion, reflection, and service. (After the prayer, turn the lights back on.)

(3) Say together the Apostles' Creed, letting the children help to lead the group in the motions they learned. (Of course, they will need someone to serve as leader.)

(4) End with the songs "Praise God, from Whom All Blessings Flow" and "We Are Faith Families" (page 117), singing along with the FaithHome tape.

Talent Checklist

_____

(NAME)

IS A CHILD OF GOD AND WAS CREATED WITH THESE GIFTS:

(Circle all the words that describe you.)

RUNNER	LIKES TO HELP	READS WELL
CAN SKIP	STRONG	LIKES MATH
KIND	BIG BROTHER/SISTER	GYMNAST
SWIMMER	KNOWS COLORS	LIKES ANIMALS
BALL PLAYER	HAPPY	LIKES FLOWERS
PLAYS AN INSTRUMENT	LOVES TO DRAW	LIKES MUSIC
LITTLE BROTHER/SISTER	MAKES BED	SINGER
LIKES EXPERIMENTS	CAN PRAY	ACOLYTE

Creation Word Search

Find and circle some of the important words from Genesis 1:1–2:3 in the puzzle below:

```
S C R E A T I O N
K Z W A T E R A U
Y B I R D S M L S
G G N T Q Z N L L
X O B H C A F Q P
G O D X M B G C T
L D N O O M Y T M
A C W M L A I E S
A N I M A L S T Z
```

Words to find:

GOD	GOOD
CREATION	BIRDS
WATER	EARTH
ANIMALS	SKY
SUN	MOON
MAN	WOMAN

Match the Pictures

Draw a line from each picture to the picture it matches.
Color the pictures if you wish.

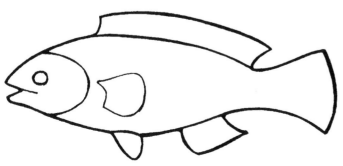

I Believe in Jesus

The streets of Moscow were almost empty, except for a few people who walked with intentional pace. It was nearly midnight. Street lights were infrequent. Car lights were absent. An American waited to catch the last subway to his hotel. A few other "last train" folk stood with him on the platform.

A young Russian standing near them phrased the question, speaking fluently in English, "Are you an American?"

"Yes," answered the American.

"Do you hate Russians?" he continued.

"No," the American said. "However, my country has been fearful and suspicious of your country."

"I know," he replied. "So it has been with us." He shifted his focus. "Are you a believer?"

"Yes, I am a Christian," the American responded.

He pressed the point: "Do you believe in Jesus?" It was as if he knew people who professed to be Christians but showed no evidence of believing in Jesus.

"Yes, I believe in Jesus. I try to follow him." The American's answers did not totally satisfy this young Russian, who became insistent.

"But *why* do you believe in Jesus?"

How would you have responded? Why do *you* believe in Jesus Christ? Write your responses below:

The American gave his questioner a forthright answer. Stating his response as clearly and carefully as possible, he said, "I believe in Jesus because he shows me who God is, who I am, and the person I can become if I will follow him."

The Russian nodded, but his questions continued: "Do you believe all the time or just when you go to a church?"

The train screeched to a halt in front of them. People pressed their way onto the cars, taking no chances on missing the last train. The Russian waved as he boarded a forward car, his last question hanging in the air as if the whole world waited to hear the answer: "Do you believe all the time or just when you go to a church?"

On a subway platform, the American affirmed, "I believe in Jesus Christ." Long ago, the earliest Christians boldly proclaimed the same belief. What does it mean?

Of the 110 words in the Apostles' Creed, 70 are about Jesus. Surprising? Hardly! Jesus is the focus of the Christian faith. The Apostles' Creed proclaims certain core truths of the Christian faith. The life, mission, message, crucifixion, and resurrection of Jesus form the bedrock of the Christian faith. Consequently, any proclamation about the Christian faith must focus on Jesus, the theme for this week.

 ## LEADER BACKGROUND MATERIAL

Conceived by the Holy Spirit, Born of the Virgin Mary

Christians believe that God initiates every relationship between a human being and God. Both the Old and New Testaments of the Bible affirm that, out of love, God chose to forge a connection with human beings.

Initially, God forged that connection through a covenant with Abraham, Sarah, and the Jewish people. This relationship was pursued through generations of their descendants, guided by the prophets and other leaders of the covenant community. Finally, at a time of God's choosing, God forged a unique bond between Creator and creature. The New Testament writers tell us that in a remarkably simple, humble, and astonishing manner, the Creator became creature.

Karl Barth—a Swiss theologian of the mid-twentieth century—wrote, "Here the hidden, the eternal and incomprehensible God has taken visible form. Here the Almighty is mighty in a quite definite, particular, earthly happening. Here the Creator Himself has become creature and therefore objective reality."[1]

The reality Christians profess is this: In Jesus, God came as a human and revealed God's self to humans. The Apostles' Creed makes these points when it proclaims that Jesus was both conceived by the Holy Spirit and born of the virgin Mary:

Jesus was completely God.
Jesus was completely human.

Which of these two points do you find more difficult to accept? Why? Write your responses below:

To minds trained to accept only those things that may be proven by hard evidence to be scientific or historic facts, the statement that Jesus was completely God may be difficult to accept. Scholars today struggle with attempts to discover who Jesus really was and what can be proven that he actually said and did. However thorough their research, their efforts will never completely satisfy everyone.

Throughout Christian history, there have been many who have tried to assert that Jesus was not truly or completely human. Because Jesus was conceived by the Holy Spirit, so the argument goes, he could not be a real human being; rather, he was a divine being and only appeared to be human. However, the view agreed upon early in the church's history through its councils is the paradox that Jesus was both divine and human. Why?

Saint Athanasius wrote in the fourth century that the paradox is due, in large part, to human need: "It was our sorry case that caused the Word to come down, our transgression that called out His love for us, so that He made haste to help us and to appear among us. It is we who were the cause of His taking human form, and for our salvation that in his great love He was both born and manifested in a human body."[2] Once again, from the early years of Christianity, the Incarnation was seen as a direct result of God's great love and ardent desire to be reconciled to human creatures. The key concept is love. Witness another declaration, this one by Saint Basil of Caesarea during the fourth century, who celebrated the transcendent God come among us: "God on earth, God among us! No longer the God who gives his law amid flashes of lightning . . . but the God who speaks gently and with kindness in a human body to his kindred."[3]

To be sure, reason and logic cannot sufficiently prove the truth of theological things. Each Christian ultimately has to decide for himself or herself what counts as reason enough to believe in Jesus' divinity and humanity.

The church's historic position, however, is that the Bible provides sufficient testimony to who Jesus was and what he means for us. In the Bible, we find accounts of a Jesus who

—was born into a human family under humble, maybe even impoverished, conditions;
—struggled with very human temptations;
—got hungry and ate, even after his resurrection;
—went away by himself for a while—perhaps out of grief, perhaps out of fear—upon hearing of the execution of John the Baptist;
—needed time alone to pray;
—cried at the death of a close friend;
—acted angrily at the sight of greed profaning the Temple of God;

—became frustrated with disciples who "didn't get it";

—really suffered and really died a painful death.

In the Bible, we also see how this very human Jesus was also very divine as he

—performed miracles, including the healing of persons with incurable ailments;

—calmed storms;

—walked on water;

—appeared "transfigured" and in the company of Moses and Elijah in a vision on a mountain before Peter, James, and John;

—taught what was in the mind of God;

—brought persons who were dead back to life;

—was himself raised by God from death.

These are things that the first generations of Christians believed about Jesus. Those who lived with him, seeing and hearing him firsthand, taught these things to others. In order to help subsequent generations know what to believe about Jesus, the church determined that the writings in what we call the New Testament authoritatively teach us the truths we need to know. The testimony of those writings uniformly proclaims the wholly divine/wholly human nature of Jesus.

What do Christians believe about "the Virgin Mary"? Christians of various theological perspectives place varying emphases upon the virginity and motherhood of Mary, with the Roman Catholic and Orthodox streams of the church elevating Mary's role more than the Protestant streams. Regardless of whether or not we agree with traditional Roman Catholic thinking, all Christian denominations value the role of Mary within the Incarnation. Elizabeth Rankin Geitz, Episcopal priest and theologian, challenges Protestants to appreciate the active role of Mary in the Incarnation when she writes, "Our call is to hear the word of God, believe it, and then to act upon that belief. In those special moments in our lives when we hear God's call to us, may we have the courage as Mary did to answer, 'Let it be with me according to your word.' "[4] To be sure, Christians of many theological persuasions can find in Mary qualities of discipleship worthy of emulation. Despite her fear upon hearing the angel's news (Luke 1:30), for example, Mary was able to accept the will of God for her life.

The New Testament speaks of the virgin birth in ways that highlight the uniqueness of Jesus and the mysterious awesomeness of God. Mary's willingness notwithstanding, the beginning of Jesus' earthly life

was an act of God. So, too, Jesus' resurrection was an act of God. The activity of God in Jesus is crucial within Christian belief.

His Only Son, Our Lord

When Jesus was baptized, Matthew reports that Jesus "saw the Spirit of God descending like a dove and alighting on him. And a voice from heaven said, 'This is my Son, the Beloved, with whom I am well pleased' " (Matthew 3:16-17). Here again we encounter the initiative of God in confirming our relationship and in giving God's very present Spirit to God's children. The Apostles' Creed speaks of Jesus as God's "only Son." What does this mean? Doesn't God have many sons and daughters?

In the Sermon on the Mount, Jesus said, "Blessed are the peacemakers, for they will be called children of God" (Matthew 5:9). Later in the sermon, Jesus asserted that loving one's enemies and praying for them will prove that you are children of your heavenly Father (Matthew 5:45). Paul, in Romans 8:14, declared that "all who are led by the Spirit of God are children of God"; and in Galatians 3:26, he stated, "For in Christ Jesus you are all children of God through faith." Likewise, in 2 Corinthians 6:18, Paul testified to God's action that claims us as daughters and sons:

> **I will be your father,**
> **and you shall be my sons and daughters.**

Surely, each believer is a child of God. Jesus, however, *perfectly* demonstrated the will of God. His teaching and lifestyle demonstrated the truth of God's kingdom and illumined the way for those who confess him to be able to follow him faithfully. Thus, the Apostles' Creed speaks of Jesus as "God's only Son, our Lord."

Suffered . . . Crucified . . . Buried

The words of the spiritual capture the truth of a fundamental perspective of the Christian faith: "Nobody knows the trouble I've seen; nobody knows but Jesus." How does Jesus know about our troubles, our suffering, our problems, our pains? Once again, Jesus can know the intimate details of human suffering because he has lived the human experience to its fullest. In his life, he scaled the heights of joy and struggled through the depths of despair and death. Jesus "suffered under Pontius Pilate, was crucified, dead, and buried."

Often our human approach to life is designed to avoid suffering and to camouflage death. Rather than seeing suffering as an inevitable part of the human journey and, therefore, developing a constructive perspective on it, we often let suffering become the occasion for bitterness, withdrawal, or rejection of ourselves and others. There is, however, an alternative.

Shortly after the end of communism in the Eastern bloc countries, a pastor visited a group of Christians working in Bulgaria. In Sophia, Bulgaria, he visited a rundown church building. Christian worship had not been held in the building for over forty years. It was heartbreaking to see the scars on the once beautiful church building, used for very different purposes while under the control of the communist government.

The pastor of the church, Zwardlo Brezlov, a man in his eighties, led the American pastor through the building. Accompanying him were a small remnant of worshipers from the old church and two new converts—young men who had construction skills. The small group of a dozen or so persons was in the process, time permitting, of restoring the beautiful old building. Simultaneously, they were rebuilding their congregational life.

The American pastor learned Pastor Brezlov's story. Over forty years earlier, he had been appointed to that congregation. Before he could preach his first sermon, however, he was arrested. Christian witness was no longer permitted. Placed in a labor camp, he endured enormous hardships for a dozen years. His health was broken, his suffering immense. Finally released, he worked as a street sweeper—hardly a challenging job for a man with advanced degrees in economics and theology. Old and frail, but with no hint of bitterness, his eyes twinkled as he recounted an event of a few months before: He preached his first sermon in his "new" appointment!

"How did you make it through all the years of suffering?" the American pastor asked. "How did you retain your joy and hope?" He would long remember the look on Pastor Brezlov's face and the strength of his voice, coming from deep within his frail body: "Jesus!"

Does a suffering Jesus help you face personal turmoil? Does a resurrected Lord empower you to live in hope that evil cannot and will not ultimately win? When have you found these statements to be true? Write your responses below:

The manner in which Jesus approached suffering and death can fill us with hope for our journey. We can affirm that he knows our need and can offer us courage to reclaim life. Into our "living hells" of daily life—anxiety, abandonment, rejection, despair, rage, and emptiness—Jesus comes. Into the living death of grief, futility, depression, separation from joy and hope and even God, Jesus comes to offer a way forward.

To say that Jesus "suffered under Pontius Pilate" is to affirm that Jesus made the journey of agony; endured unjust treatment; and experienced the loneliness of rejection by his own faith community, including desertion by the very followers he loved and supported. Jesus experienced the assault of life's harshest treatment and risked his life for faith, even at the price of great suffering. Little wonder that the New Testament writers saw in Jesus the realization of Israel's messianic hope!

The Christian faith is clear and confident. Jesus did not merely seem human or come into our midst as a God dressed up in skin. Jesus was fully human—so human, in fact, that he "suffered under Pontius Pilate"; so human that he died. Jesus experienced that moment when the destructive freedom of the forces of nation, religion, and popular tyranny were hurled against him. The solitariness of the unalterable march in the abyss of death was inevitable. "It is finished" (John 19:30). Jesus died. The death of Jesus removed all barriers between God and humanity. "And he died for all, so that those who live might live no longer for themselves, but for him who died" (2 Corinthians 5:15).

Several years ago a family visited a theme park where they rode in little cars through a darkened tunnel. They sped toward the shadows of a "dead end," each of them feeling his or her own level of fear and anxiety about the unknown rising sharply. When it seemed they were about to smash into a wall, a sudden turn, a shaft of light, and a way forward offered themselves to the family. Jesus is that way forward for Christians!

He Rose from the Dead

Of what importance is the Resurrection to Christians? The apostle Paul gives us a hint: "If Christ has not been raised, then our proclamation has been in vain and your faith has been in vain. . . . But in fact, Christ has been raised from the dead" (1 Corinthians 15:14, 20).

The disciples of Jesus and a steadily growing number of persons who confessed their faith in Jesus Christ as Lord and Savior spread across the world, proclaiming with passion and conviction, "Jesus Christ is the living Lord." So strong was their conviction that they were willing to face hungry beasts and bloodthirsty, jeering mobs. They risked everything to gather secretly to worship and witness to their faith, summarized simply in three words: He is risen! Although there is some variety in the way the four Gospels describe the Resurrection, there is complete agreement among them as to its central importance. Each writer was clear that Jesus was alive.

The resurrection of Jesus was absolutely real to the followers of Jesus, but not because Jesus was simply found to be absent from the tomb. The Resurrection was absolutely real because Jesus was present in their midst. The cross was not the end of Jesus' presence or transforming love. The tomb, empty or occupied, stirred no hopes and provoked no assurances. It was the living Christ, this Jesus whom God raised from the dead, that baffled and beckoned early Christians. "We have seen the Lord," they said (John 20:25). The disciple Thomas, captive to a strong dose of realism and his own brand of scientific verification, abandoned every ounce of skepticism in the midst of

the living Christ. He shamelessly and confidently exclaimed, "My Lord and my God" (John 20:28).

Their Eyes Were Opened

One of the most engaging descriptions of the Resurrection appearances is Luke's account of the walk to Emmaus in Luke 24:13-35. In that encounter, the living Christ became known to two followers when they shared a meal together.

It is no accident that some of the most faith-formative experiences happen during fellowship at the table. The Jews, for example, practice a kind of "table spirituality"[5] in which the home, rather than the synagogue, is the locus for major holy days. It was within the context of a family Passover meal that Jesus introduced the sacrament of the Lord's Supper. It was within homes that the early church gathered to bear witness to growing faith in their Lord and Savior and to share in the Eucharist. It is at the family "altar"—the kitchen or dining room table— where family bonds can be strengthened and faith insights can best be shared during the FaithHome experience. The weekly meal during this experience is intentionally reflective of the Emmaus meal— when "nourishment" had little to do with the food eaten and everything to do with "eyes becoming open."

What meaning does the Emmaus event have for you?

As you prepare to lead this session, in what ways have your "eyes become opened"? Record your thoughts below:

LEADER'S WEEKLY SESSION GUIDE

Week 3: I Believe in Jesus

Objectives:

By the end of the session, adults and children will have

—learned a story in the Bible told by Jesus;
—stated questions and beliefs about Jesus;
—worshiped God together, thanking God for Jesus;
—explored Jesus as fully human and fully divine.

Materials Needed:

For Full Group: FaithHome video, video player and monitor, family banners, construction paper, scissors, crayons and markers, cross patterns (page 48), glue, fabric glue, fabric paints, Christ candle, matches, audio tape player, FaithHome tape

For Adults: copies of the Apostles' Creed (page 25, or use copies from previous weeks), newsprint, markers, tape, writing paper, pencils or pens, *Family Guides*

For Children: signing motions for the Apostles' Creed (page 24), yarn, black construction paper, black crayons, pencils, thin white or yellow washable paint, large paintbrushes, Bibles, audio tape player and cassette tape (see Activity 3), FaithHome tape, posters and pictures of Jesus and events in Jesus' life (for example, old bulletin covers and Sunday school curriculum; see Activities 1 and 2), pictures of crosses (see Activity 1), 9" x 12" posterboard for each child, crayons and markers, glue, scissors, copies of "A Secret Message" for older children (page 49), copies of "Find Jesus" for younger children (page 50)

Welcome (3 minutes)

Welcome the group and thank them for being present for this third session of FaithHome. Ask one person from each family to share one thing they enjoyed from their "Family Faith Breaks" or "Family Meals" during the past week.

Video Segment (10 minutes)

Introduce the video segment by saying something like this:

This week we will be talking about Jesus. Let's see what our friends on the video have to say. As you watch, think about how you would answer the questions. We will talk about that briefly after viewing the segment.

After playing the video segment, allow a few minutes for discussion (see page 11 for a list of questions to encourage discussion).

Group Activity (15 minutes)

This week each family will make a cross, representing Jesus, to add to their family banner. On each table, place family banners, construction paper, scissors, cross patterns (page 48), fabric glue, and crayons and markers. Instruct each family to cut a cross out of construction paper. Then they are to draw pictures and symbols or to write words on the cross to show what they believe about Jesus. When they are done, they can glue the cross to their family banner. Allow 15 minutes for the families to work together. Tell them that they will be sharing something about their crosses during the closing time.

Adult Session (40-45 minutes)

(1) Repeat the questions from the video segment and allow the adults briefly to share their ideas.

—What do you think about Jesus?
—If Jesus were here today, what would he do?
—What's your favorite story about Jesus?
—What would you say to Jesus if you were face to face?

OR

Invite them to talk about their experiences at home during the previous week. (5 minutes)

(2) Hand out copies of the Apostles' Creed (page 25; use the same copies from previous weeks, if you like), along with white paper, pencils or pens, and markers. Ask the group to read all the way through the creed and then reread the statement about Jesus. Have each person draw a picture or symbol that sums up what he or she believes about Jesus. (5 minutes)

(3) When all have finished, ask them to lay their pictures face up on a common table. Then ask the group:

What are some of the things these pictures show that we know or affirm about Jesus?

Record responses on newsprint. (2-5 minutes)

(4) Say to the group:

What do you most remember about the "Background Basics" for Week 3 that you read in your **Family Guide?** *As I review the background material for this week, I'd like to include points that had real meaning for you, questions that occurred to you as you read this material, or stories from your life or that of your children that you thought of as you read the material.*

Record on newsprint any questions that you may address together. (2-5 minutes)

(5) Summarize the "Leader's Background Material" for Week 3, being sure to include the following points:

—Jesus is the focus of the Christian faith.
—Jesus is truly God and truly human. This has been a difficult concept for the church from its beginning.
—We know Jesus is human because
  • Jesus was born to a human family.
  • Jesus was tempted.
  • Jesus got hungry and ate.
  • Jesus cried.
  • Jesus prayed.
  • Jesus was frustrated.
  • Jesus suffered and died.
  (For each of these statements, ask for a Scripture story or reference that helps us know this.)
—We know Jesus was divine because
  • Jesus walked on water.
  • Jesus calmed the storm.
  • Jesus healed.
  • Jesus brought persons back from death.
  • Jesus was resurrected.
  (Again, ask for Scripture references from the group for each statement.)
—We believe in the resurrection of Jesus, even though we may not understand all that it means. (10 minutes)

(6) Go back to the group's questions listed earlier and briefly answer any that have not been addressed. Invite responses from the group. When answering, try to move the group to reflection on what they

think and feel their children's questions about Jesus will be. (5 minutes)

(7) Spend additional time on the concepts of death, dying, and resurrection. Have the participants break into pairs and choose one question that a child might have that is related to these concepts for the whole group to answer. Take these questions one at a time. As the group discusses the questions, remind them of the following guidelines for answering a child's questions:

—Remember the age of the child. The younger the child, the shorter the response should be.
—Know the life experience of the child. If a child has lost a loved one, that child is more likely to wonder about heaven and the afterlife and to ask direct questions.
—Assure the child that there are some things we do not know entirely, but we know God loves us and God's plans are good.
—Stay true to your own beliefs. Use statements such as, "I believe" or "In my experience." Then ask the child what he or she believes.
—Instead of trying to think of an answer to a particular question, ask the child what he or she thinks and really listen. (10 minutes)

Children's Session (40-45 minutes)

Opening Circle (8 minutes)

Invite the children to sit with you in a circle. Play the web game. Explain the game in the following way:

I have a ball of yarn here. I am going to unwind some of the yarn and toss it to one of you in the circle. Before I toss it, I will say, "God loves you, (say name of child)." When you catch the ball, unwind some of the yarn. Hold on to your part; then toss the ball to someone else. You have to say, "God loves you" and the name of the person before you toss the ball. Always toss the ball to someone who doesn't already have a piece of yarn.

Play the game. When all the children have had the ball tossed to them, ask the last child to toss it back to you. Then say:

We are going to place our yarn web on the floor carefully and see what we have created.

Look at the web together and say:

This is a beautiful creation. God loves each of you. I'm glad you're here today to learn more about God and Jesus.

Ask the children:

What did you think about the video we watched?

Take a few statements from the group. Add statements of your own to help the children reflect on what they saw.

Show the children the activities that they will be doing.

Activity One: Art Center (8 minutes)

Surprise Pictures

For Older Children: Post pictures or posters of Jesus where the children can see them. Also post pictures of crosses that you have drawn. Say to the children:

We can look at these pictures of Jesus and remember things we know about Jesus. We can look at the crosses and remember Jesus because the cross is a symbol that Christians everywhere use. Today each of you is going to create a "surprise picture" of Jesus or of a cross.

Hand each child a sheet of black construction paper, a pencil, and a black crayon. Instruct the children to think about what kind of picture each of them will draw. Tell them to use pencils to draw their pictures on black construction paper. Then have them go over their drawings with black crayons, pressing down really hard.

Have ready a thin, runny mixture of white or yellow paint (use washable paint) and large paintbrushes. Instruct the children to brush a thin coat of paint over the surface of their pictures, causing them to appear "magically"!

For Younger Children: Younger children may not be able to draw a picture. Let them make designs instead on crosses you have pre-cut from black construction paper. Help them press hard with their crayons and then paint over their pictures to see them appear. As the children work, talk together about the pictures or posters of Jesus and what the children know about Jesus.

Activity Two: Discovery Center (8 minutes)

"Jesus Is" Collages

For Older Children: Display pictures of events from Jesus' life—Jesus' birth, Jesus as a boy, Jesus teaching, Jesus healing, Jesus praying, Jesus on the cross, Jesus' resurrection. After the children have looked at all the pictures, have them create their own collages of Jesus' life. Provide a 9" x 12" posterboard for each child, pictures of Jesus' life from old bulletin covers and Sunday school curriculum, scissors, glue, and crayons and markers. Instruct the children to write "JESUS IS" in the center of their posterboard and then to glue or draw pictures around the words to show who they know Jesus to be.

For Younger Children: Print "JESUS IS" on the posterboard in advance. Provide some pre-cut pictures as well as some that they can cut out and glue themselves. (Glue sticks work well with younger children.)

Activity Three: Study Center (10 minutes)

For Older Children: Distribute Bibles. Post the following Scriptures on posterboard for the children to see: Luke 2:41-49; Mark 10:13-16. Tell half of the children to read the passage from Luke and the other half to read the passage from Mark. After each child has read his or her passage, instruct each of them to find another child who did not read that story and to tell the story to him or her. After every child has told a story and heard a story, hand out copies of "A Secret Message" (page 49). Let them help one another decipher the secret message.

For Younger Children: Prepare in advance an audio recording of someone reading Mark 10:13-16. Let the children listen to the story of Jesus and the children. Distribute copies of "Find Jesus" (page 50). Show the children how to connect the dots to find the picture of Jesus. Then they may color the picture with crayons or markers.

Closing Circle (10 Minutes)

Call the children together in a circle. Let each child share one thing he or she has learned or done. Summarize with the children what we know about Jesus, including the following points:

—Jesus was someone who taught that learning about God is important.

—Jesus loved children and told adults they need to trust and believe like children.

—Jesus believed each person is important to God.

—Jesus taught that we are to worship and praise God.

—Jesus died on the cross but was resurrected by God.

Using the poster on page 24, lead the children in signing the Apostles' Creed. Concentrate on the motions as you say the words. Encourage those who can read to say the words along with you. Remember, children often learn one skill at a time; do not worry if they cannot match the words with the motions. Let them follow with their hands as you say the words. Tell the children they will be helping to lead the adults in these signs in a few minutes.

Listen to "Jesus, Our Friend," "Jesus Loves Me," and/or "When Jesus Came to Jerusalem" on the FaithHome tape and then sing along. End with a brief prayer of thanks for this learning time together.

CLOSING TIME (15 minutes)

(1) As the children and adults come together, ask the adults to go with their children back to the tables where they worked on their crosses. Invite each family to share one thing from their crosses that tells something they believe about Jesus.

(2) After every family has had a chance to speak, ask the group to enter with you into a brief time of prayer. Light the Christ candle; then dim the lights. Pray, asking for God's guidance for each family present and for strength to continue the commitment of study, discussion, reflection, and service. (After the prayer, turn the lights back on.)

(3) Say together the Apostle's Creed, letting the children help to lead the group in the motions they are learning.

(4) End with the songs "Jesus, Our Friend" and "Jesus Loves Me," singing along with the FaithHome tape.

48

A Secret Message

The scrambled words below are found in John 3:16 (NRSV).
Unscramble the words and put the numbered letters in the spaces at the bottom of the page.
Then read the message to find out what we can be.

RFO   DGO   OS   VLOED   ETH   RWDLO   HTTA

___ ___   ___ ___ ___   ___ ___   ___ ___ ___ ___ ___   ___ ___ ___   ___ ___ ___ ___ ___   ___ ___ ___ ___
3 1   8   4   9   2

EH   VGEA   SHI   NYLO   NOS,   OS   TTAH

___ ___   ___ ___ ___ ___   ___ ___ ___   ___ ___ ___ ___   ___ ___ ___,   ___ ___   ___ ___ ___ ___
                      5   12

YREEVEON   HWO   IBEEELSV   NI   MHI   YMA

___ ___ ___ ___ ___ ___ ___ ___   ___ ___ ___   ___ ___ ___ ___ ___ ___ ___   ___ ___   ___ ___ ___   ___ ___ ___
                          7

TNO   RPSHEI   TUB   YMA   VHEA   TREEANL

___ ___ ___   ___ ___ ___ ___ ___ ___   ___ ___ ___   ___ ___ ___   ___ ___ ___ ___   ___ ___ ___ ___ ___ ___ ___
13   6   10

FELI.

___ ___ ___ ___
11

___ ___ ___ ___ , ___ ___ ___ ___ ___ ___ ___ ___ ___ ___
8 1 4 5   3 12 11 2 7 9 6 10 12

49

Find Jesus

Connect the dots
from **1 to 12**
to find Jesus.

Color the picture.

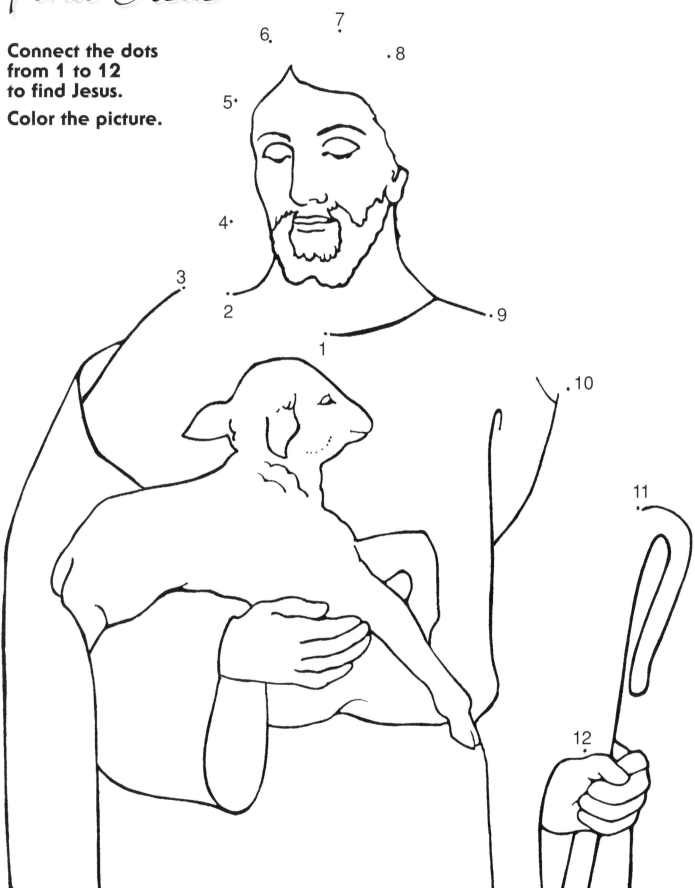

50

I Believe in the Holy Spirit

Who is the Holy Spirit? What images are invoked in our minds when we refer to "the Spirit"? What does it mean to proclaim, as Christians have for centuries, "I believe in the Holy Spirit"? How can we help our children to understand the difficult concept of the Holy Spirit? These are some of the questions we will be exploring during this fourth week of FaithHome.

 ## LEADER BACKGROUND MATERIAL

Images of the Spirit

Scholars tell us that the writers of both the Old and the New Testament use words meaning "wind" when they speak of the Holy Spirit. The Hebrew word *ruach* means "spirit," as does the Greek word *pneuma*. The pronouncement of the first of these words puts one in touch with the forcefulness of the Spirit, for *ruach* is spoken almost gutturally (ROO-auhk). Force, energy, wind, fire—these are some of the traditional images used for the Spirit. Let us consider these and other images chosen by the biblical writers and the possible reasons for their choices.

The Spirit has been imaged as force, or energy—moving, creating, life giving. The concept of the Holy Spirit as force and energy is critical within Christianity, where the Spirit is linked to "second birth." One of the earliest statements of the Christian faith says, "We believe in the Holy Spirit, the Lord, the giver of life."[1] In John's Gospel, Nicodemus asks Jesus, "Can one enter a second time into the mother's womb and be born?" (3:4). In the following verse we read, "Jesus answered, 'Very truly, I tell you, no one can enter the kingdom of God without being born of water and Spirit' " (3:5). Birth—our physical birth and our spiritual birth—requires force and energy!

The Spirit has been imaged as wind—necessary for breathing, sometimes gentle, sometimes forceful, always with us. It is the air we breathe—the very means by which the whole creation lives and breathes. We cannot see the wind, but we can feel its presence and remain aware of its power. These insights into the concept of "wind" enabled the biblical writers to declare basic insights about the Spirit. It is God's presence and power always, continually, in our midst. "When the day of Pentecost had come, they were all gathered together in one place. And suddenly from heaven there came a sound like the rush of a violent wind, and it filled the entire house where they were sitting" (Acts 2:1-2).

The Spirit has been imaged as fire—powerful, helpful, dangerous, delightful to behold, warming, energizing. The writer of Acts records that on the first Pentecost, "divided tongues, as of fire, appeared among them, and a tongue rested on each of them" (Acts 2:3). The results were fascinating! All of a sudden, communication was enhanced as believers were able to share the good news of the gospel in a variety of languages, enabling persons of diverse cultures and backgrounds to hear the story of a resurrected Lord and believe. Just as the small flame from a struck match spreads in a fireplace when air and kindling come together, resulting in a roaring fire, so also the fire of the Spirit kindled "the zeal of Christ's followers waiting in Jerusalem for his promised gift."[2]

How do you think of the Holy Spirit? Does one image—more than others—capture for you the meaning of the Spirit? If you were going to "re-image" the Holy Spirit, what images would freshly capture its reality? Write your responses below:

One in Three Persons

It is important for us to understand that when we say, "I believe in the Holy Spirit," we are declaring again our belief in God and Jesus. How? The Holy Spirit did not arrive on the scene in a kind of chronological order that began with God, continued with Jesus, and culminated in the Holy Spirit. The Holy Spirit was not given for the first time at Pentecost; the Old Testament speaks frequently of God's Spirit poured out for guidance, wisdom, and faithfulness. The first chapter of Genesis describes the Spirit's creative action: "A wind from God swept over the face of the waters" (1:2). The Spirit is constantly present; we cannot flee from it (see Psalm 139:7). Jesus referred to the life-giving power of the Spirit (see Luke 4:18). Later, the Acts of the Apostles celebrated the Spirit's power to gather and energize the church, while Paul's writings spoke confidently of the Spirit as God's present power for the faithfulness and fruitfulness of the Christian life.

The Nicene Creed helps us to understand early Christian beliefs: "We believe in the Holy Spirit, the Lord, the giver of life." Associating the two—Holy Spirit and Lord—means that the Holy Spirit is equal to God. Paul said it well: "Now the Lord is the Spirit" (2 Corinthians 3:17). Likewise, Saint Basil of Caesarea wrote, "The Lord has delivered to us a necessary and saving dogma: The Holy Spirit is to be ranked with the Father . . . in everything the Holy Spirit is indivisibly and inseparably joined to the Father and the Son. . . the Holy Spirit partakes of the fullness of divinity."[3]

So the traditional understanding of Christians is that of unity in the Godhead—literally three persons of one substance, power, and eternity. The role of the Spirit within the Trinity is to energize Christian believers for missional faithfulness—nothing less than the re-presenting of Jesus' ministry in our time and place. The Spirit brings us assurance that the work of Christ's mission has been entrusted to us. The very presence of God will uphold us in the doing of Christ's work.

How have you felt empowered by the Holy Spirit to do Christ's work? Record your thoughts by writing a letter of thanksgiving on a separate sheet of paper.

Another Look at the Trinity

The Trinity is the church's way of talking about how God is God. It can be a bit confusing! In fact, coming to this understanding challenged the early church for many years, finally ending in the statements we affirm in the Apostles' Creed and Nicene Creed. Perhaps we can grasp the fullness behind the concept by using two—notably flawed—analogies.

One analogy is that of water in various forms of being. It may begin as water (the substance of God). It may emerge as ice cubes (Jesus)—a notably different form of the same substance. When boiled on the stove, ice cubes will turn to steam (Holy Spirit)—the same substance of the same water, now released with spewing energy into the air.

Consider a second analogy. A parent can be, simultaneously, a mother, daughter, and grandmother. True, the expressions are different, but the substance is the same.

What other analogies might you offer to explain the Trinity? Make notes below:

Elizabeth Rankin Geitz reminds us of the difficulty Christians have—and always have had—when they attempt to speak about the Trinity:

> A fifteenth-century Flemish painting in the series "Scenes from the Life of Augustine," depicts a boy sitting on the beach. He has dug a hole in the sand and is trying to fill it with water. St. Augustine, as legend has it, says to the boy, "Young man, don't you realize what you're attempting is an impossible task?" The boy replies, "Don't you realize that trying to write about the Trinity is an impossible task?"[4]

Impossible task, unfathomable mystery—however one attempts to explain it, the doctrine of the Trinity provides us with a summary of the fullness of God. Our focus on the Holy Spirit keeps us conscious of the personal nearness of God for each of us. Ultimately, God is intimately involved with us, as the Spirit of the risen Christ.

What Difference Does it Make?

Weeks 1-4 of FaithHome have focused on the meaning of the Trinity. Take a few moments now to reflect on the implications this focus on the Trinity may have for your life and for the lives of the families in your FaithHome group.

In the space below, draw a triangle. Label the points "Father," "Son," and "Holy Spirit." Reflect on what each title means to you and your relationship with God.

Now draw another triangle. Label this triangle with other words you also use to describe the Trinity, such as "Creator," "Redeemer," "Sustainer," or the titles Augustine describes in his book *De Trinitate*: "Lover," "Beloved," "Love."

What implications for Christian families does our study of the Trinity hold? Write your reflections below:

 ## LEADER'S WEEKLY SESSION GUIDE

Week 4: I Believe in the Holy Spirit

Objectives:

By the end of the session, children and adults will have

—talked together about what "God with us" means;
—read or heard the story of the coming of the Holy Spirit at Pentecost;
—worshiped God through song and prayer.

 Materials Needed:

For Full Group: FaithHome video, video player and monitor, family banners, construction paper, scissors, markers, flame patterns (page 58), glue, fabric glue, red glitter, Christ candle, matches, cassette tape player, FaithHome tape

For Adults: copies of the Apostles' Creed (page 25, or use copies from previous weeks), newsprint, markers, tape, writing paper, pencils or pens, *Family Guides*

For Children: signing motions for the Apostles' Creed (page 24); Bibles; cassette tape player and cassette tape (see Activity 3); FaithHome tape; red, orange, and yellow tissue paper; flame pattern; glue; scissors; balloons; cloth handkerchiefs; four 12-inch threads for each child; white construction paper and other white paper; craft sticks or paintbrushes; crayons and markers; small boxes; acetate sheets; cellophane tape; colorful scarves; copies of "A Coded Message" (page 59) and "What Helps Me Know God Is Near" (page 60)

Welcome (3 minutes)

Welcome the group and thank them for being here for this fourth session of FaithHome. Ask one person from each family to share one thing they enjoyed from their "Family Faith Breaks" or "Family Meals" during the past week.

Video Segment (10 minutes)

Introduce the video segment by saying something like this:

This week we will be talking about the Holy Spirit. Let's see what our friends on the video have to say. As you watch, think about how you would answer the questions. We will talk about that briefly after viewing the segment.

After playing the video segment, allow a few minutes for discussion (see page 11 for a list of questions to encourage discussion).

Group Activity (15 minutes)

This week each family will make a flame, representing the Holy Spirit, to add to their family banner. On each table, place family banners, construction paper, flame patterns, glue, fabric glue, red glitter, and scissors. Ask each family to use glue and glitter to decorate their flames, which symbolize the Holy Spirit. Encourage the families to talk about what it means to them to know that God is near. Allow 15 minutes for the families to complete their flames and to glue them to their family banners. Tell the families that they will be sharing something about their flames during the closing time.

Adult Session (40-45 minutes)

(1) Repeat one or more of the questions from the video segment and allow the adults briefly to share their ideas.

—Who is the Holy Spirit?
—How would you describe the Holy Spirit?
—How would you describe the Holy Spirit's presence in your life?

OR

Invite them to talk about their experiences at home during the previous week. (5 minutes)

(2) Hand out copies of the Apostles' Creed (page 25; use the same copies from previous weeks, if you like). Ask the group to read all the way through the creed and then reread the statement about the Holy Spirit. Instruct each person to write the words "HOLY SPIRIT" down the side of the paper or on the back. For each of the letters in the words *Holy Spirit*, they are to think of a word or phrase that says something about what they believe about the Holy Spirit. Tell them to write the first word or phrase that comes to mind. Print one example on newsprint to help participants understand the instructions. (For instance, the word for the letter "L" could be "Living.") After a few minutes, let the group complete the acrostic you began on newsprint. (5-7 minutes)

(3) Invite the participants to share questions they think their children might ask about the Holy Spirit. List the questions on newsprint. Tell them you will come back to these questions later. (3 minutes)

(4) Say to the group:

What do you most remember about the "Background Basics" for Week 4 that you read in your **Family Guide**? *As I review the background material for this week, I'd like to include points that had real meaning for you, questions that occurred to you as you read this material, or stories from your life or the lives of your children that you thought of as you read the material.*

Record on newsprint any questions that you may address together. (2-5 minutes)

(5) Summarize the "Leader's Background Material" for Week 4, being sure to include the following points:

—In both the Old Testament and the New Testament, words meaning "wind" are used for the word *Spirit*. In Hebrew the word is *ruach*. In Greek the word is *pneuma*.
—Images of the Spirit include force, energy, wind, and fire.

—Although we most often associate the Holy Spirit with Pentecost, God as Spirit occurs in many other places in the Bible. (You might read from Acts 2, as well as from Genesis 1:2, Psalm 139:7, and Luke 4:18.)
—Spirit is also used to signify our spiritual birth. Remind the group of the story of Nicodemus.
—The role of the Spirit is to energize us.
—The Spirit gives us the assurance that God is near.
—The members of the Trinity are of the same substance but are different forms of the One God. (10 minutes)

(6) Go back to the group's questions listed earlier and briefly answer any that have not been addressed. Invite responses from the group. When answering, try to move the group to reflection on what they think and feel their children's questions about the Trinity will be. (5 minutes)

(7) Instruct each person to find a partner. Assign each pair one question from the list of children's questions. Let them decide together what an appropriate response to this question might be. Listen to all the questions and responses as a group. (10 minutes)

Children's Session (40-45 minutes)

Opening Circle (5-10 minutes)

Invite the children to sit with you in a circle. Play a name game. Say to the children:

We're going to take a trip to Jerusalem! All of you are invited to come along, but you can bring only one thing. Whatever you bring has to start with the first letter of your name. So if Bobby were coming with us, he could bring a bat. We'll start with (name of child to your right). She will say her name and tell us what she would bring. Now it gets harder. The next person has to say his name and what he's bringing and then say the name of his neighbor and what she's bringing. We're going to go all around the circle trying to remember everyone's name and what they're bringing. Don't worry—we'll help one another remember.

Play the game, ending with you saying all the names of the children and what they will be bringing. Tell the children that although we will not really be going to Jerusalem, we will be hearing about something that happened in Jerusalem that helps us learn about the Holy Spirit.

Ask the children:

What did you think about the video we watched?

Take a few statements from the group. Add statements of your own to help the children reflect on what they saw.

Show the children the activities that they will be doing.

Activity One: Art Center (10 minutes)

Floating Flames

For Older Children: Provide red, orange, and yellow tissue paper; flame patterns (page 58); scissors; cellophane tape; small boxes (one for each child); and sheets of acetate (one for each child). Instruct each child to use crayons or markers to color the inside of his or her box. Then have the child use a pattern to cut five or six flames from various colors of tissue paper. Next tell the children to twist their flames in the middle and put them inside the box. Have each child place a piece of acetate over the box, cut it so that it completely covers the opening, and tape it in place. Now show the children how to rub their hands over the acetate, causing the flames to jump and "float."

For Younger Children: Ask an older child to work as a partner with a younger child. Trace enough flame patterns onto tissue paper for all the younger children in advance so that the children can cut them out and twist them. (Or do all three steps in advance.) Have the older children help the younger children complete their floating flames.

OR

Flame Stained Glass Windows

For All Children: Provide flame patterns; red, orange, and yellow tissue paper; glue; and white construction paper. Have the children trace a flame pattern onto a sheet of white construction paper and cut it out. (Prepare these in advance for younger children.) Then have them use craft sticks or paint brushes to cover their flames with a thick layer of glue. Now have the children tear various colors of tissue paper into small bits and glue them to the flame. (Young children will need some assistance.)

Talk about how stained glass windows in our churches often remind us of God, Jesus, and the Holy Spirit.

Activity Two: Discovery Center (5 minutes)

Choose one of the activities below and have fun experimenting with wind and air!

Floating Parachutes

For Older Children: Provide a handkerchief and four 12-inch pieces of thread for each child. Show the children how to tie a thread to each corner of the handkerchief, bringing the threads together and tying them in the center. Encourage the children to experiment by throwing the handkerchiefs into the air and watching them float down.

For Younger Children: Prepare the parachutes in advance and let the children have fun tossing them into the air!

Note: *If time permits, all children can decorate their parachutes with markers.*

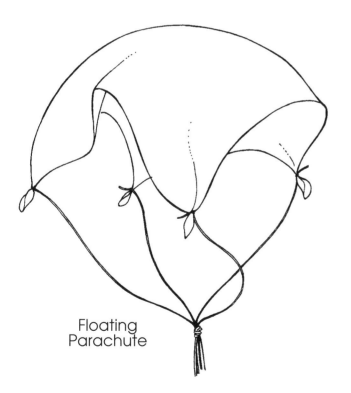

Floating Parachute

Balloon Toss

For All Children: Provide balloons for the children. Let the children blow up the balloons and then let the balloons go. (You will need to blow up the balloons for younger children, or ask the older children to help the younger children.) Tell the children to watch what happens to the "wind" inside the balloons.

As the children experiment, talk with them about the wind that allows the parachutes to float down and the balloons to float around the room. Ask:

Can you see the wind? How do you know it's there? How do you know that the wind has power?

Paper Fans

For All Children: Give each child an 8½" x 11" piece of paper. Have the children decorate their papers on both sides, using crayons or markers. Then show the children how to "accordion fold" their papers, turning up one end when folded. (Younger children will need assistance.) Now let them spread their fans and enjoy fanning themselves and one another!

Activity Three: Study Center (10 minutes)

For Older Children: Distribute Bibles. Instruct the children to choose one of the following passages of Scripture: Acts 2:1-4; Genesis 1:1-5; Psalm 139:1-10; or 2 Corinthians 3:17-18. After each child has read one of these passages of Scripture, tell them that each person is to draw the image of the Holy Spirit described in the passage he or she read. Distribute copies of "A Coded Message" (page 59). Ask the children to find the Scripture message by using the code.

For Younger Children: Prepare in advance an audio recording of someone reading Acts 2:1-4. Let the children listen to the story of the coming of the Spirit at Pentecost. Then have them move like the wind, waving colorful scarves, as music plays. Distribute copies of "What Helps Me Know God Is Near" (page 60). Let the children circle the pictures of things that help them know God is near.

Closing Circle (10 minutes)

Call the children together in a circle. Let each child share one thing he or she has learned or done.

Summarize with the children what we know about the Holy Spirit, including the following points:

—The Holy Spirit is that part of God that helps us know God is always with us.
—At Pentecost, the Holy Spirit appeared as wind and fire.
—We use the flame to symbolize the Holy Spirit.

Using the poster on page 24, lead the children in signing the Apostles' Creed. Concentrate on the motions while you say the words. Encourage those who can read to say the words along with you. Remember, children often learn one skill at a time; do not worry if they cannot match the words with the motions. Let them follow with their hands as you say the words. Tell the children they will be helping to lead the adults in these signs in a few minutes.

Listen to "Prayer Song" and/or "I Was Glad" on the FaithHome tape and then sing along. End with a brief prayer of thanks for this learning time together.

Closing Time (15 minutes)

(1) As the children and adults come together, ask the adults to go with their children back to the tables where they worked on their flames. Invite each family to show their flame to the group and tell one thing they have learned about the Holy Spirit.

(2) After every family has had a chance to speak, ask the group to enter with you into a brief time of prayer. Light the Christ candle; then dim the lights. Pray, asking for God's guidance for each family present and for strength to continue the commitment of study, discussion, reflection, and service. (After the prayer, turn the lights back on.)

(3) Say together the Apostles' Creed, letting the children help to lead the group in the motions they are learning.

(4) End with the songs "Come! Come! Everybody Worship!" and "We Are Faith Families" (page 117), singing along with the FaithHome tape.

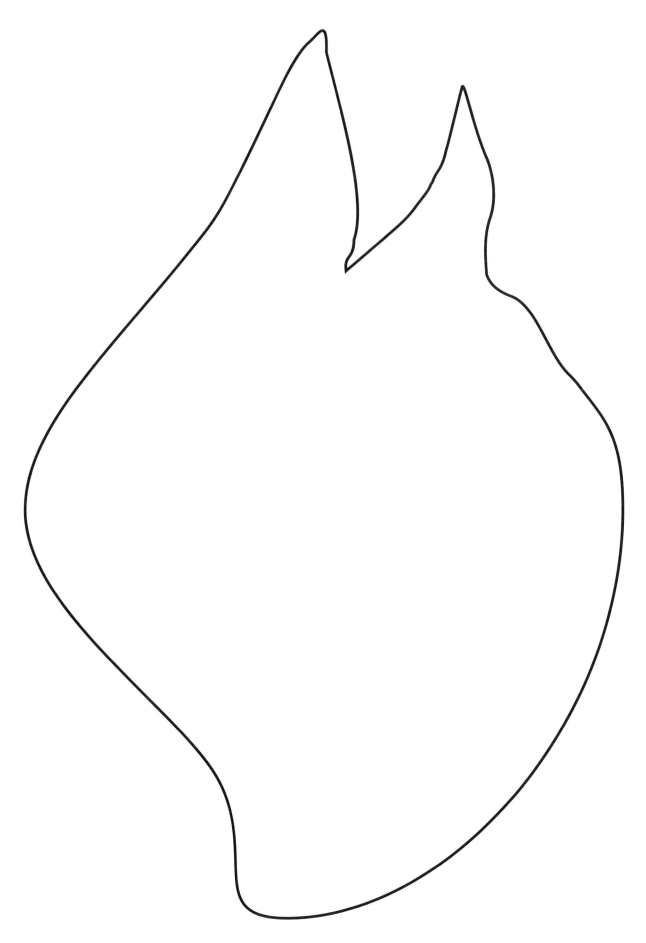

A Coded Message

Use the following key to decode the blessing of God, Jesus, and the Holy Spirit.
Then find 2 Corinthians 13:13 in your Bible (NRSV) to check your answer.

A	B	C	D	E	F	G	H	I	J	K	L	M	N	O	P
26	25	24	23	22	21	20	19	18	17	16	15	14	13	12	11

Q	R	S	T	U	V	W	X	Y	Z
10	9	8	7	6	5	4	3	2	1

___ ___ ___   ___ ___ ___ ___ ___   ___ ___   ___ ___ ___   ___ ___ ___ ___
7 19 22   20 9 26 24 22   12 21   7 19 22   15 12 9 23

___ ___ ___ ___ ___   ___ ___ ___ ___ ___ ___,   ___ ___ ___
17 22 8 6 8   24 19 9 18 8 7   7 19 22

___ ___ ___ ___   ___ ___   ___ ___ ___,   ___ ___ ___   ___ ___ ___
15 12 5 22   12 21   20 12 23   26 13 23   7 19 22

___ ___ ___ ___ ___ ___ ___ ___ ___   ___ ___
24 12 14 14 6 13 18 12 13   12 21

___ ___ ___   ___ ___ ___ ___   ___ ___ ___ ___ ___ ___   ___ ___   ___ ___ ___ ___
7 19 22   19 12 15 2   8 11 18 9 18 7   25 22   4 18 7 19

___ ___ ___   ___ ___   ___ ___ ___.
26 15 15   12 21   2 12 6

What Helps Me Know
God Is Near

Circle the pictures of things that help you know God is near.
Color the pictures.

We Are a Learning Church

Several years ago a pastor began a new congregation. As is often the case, the temporary meeting place for the newly formed congregation was an elementary school located fairly close to the future site of the church building. One Sunday the pastor was greeting those who had attended the worship service. It was then that he overheard a comment from the four-year-old son of a visiting family. The child announced authoritatively, "Well, I'll tell you one thing. They sure built that church to look like a school!"

As clever as that little boy's comment was, it illustrates a common, ongoing misconception about the nature and mission of the church. Say the word *church*, and most people will respond in "place and time" language—complete with name and address. Many of us automatically use the word *church* to refer to a building. When children hear the comment, "I'm going to the church," they understand that an individual is going to a specific location. Yet, seldom does the Scripture envision brick and mortar (or acrylic and steel!) when it refers to church.

Trevor Huddleston, in his book *I Believe: Reflections on the Creed*, writes,

> In the Bible, out of all the chapters and verses where the word occurs, only once (and that is in the Old Testament) does it refer to a building. The original word, first in Hebrew, then in Greek and Latin, means "called"—or rather "called out." The Church in which we are professing our belief is always people . . . people who are "called out" by God for a purpose.

For the next three weeks, we will explore what we mean when we speak of the church. This week we focus on the church as a learning community and what this means for individuals and families within the church family. In Week 6 we will explore the role of the church as a worshiping community. In Week 7 we will examine the prophetic role of the church as a witnessing and serving community. And in none of these weeks will we talk of the church as a building!

Composers Avery and Marsh celebrate the diverse, "called out" nature of the Christian church in their beautiful hymn "We Are the Church" (see page 119), which you will sing during your FaithHome gathering this week. The refrain of the hymn says it well:

> I am the church! You are the church!
> We are the church together!
> All who follow Jesus, all around the world!
> Yes, we're the church together![2]

The church is a specific kind of people. Who are these people? What do they believe? How do they live out the true calling of the church? These are some of the questions we will be exploring this week.

 ## LEADER BACKGROUND MATERIAL

I Believe in the Holy Catholic Church, the Communion of Saints

Throughout our FaithHome experience, we have used the Apostles' Creed as a kind of "backdrop" for our study. You have used the creed in every FaithHome gathering. Each family has taken home a copy of the creed to put on their dinner table or in another central location. Many, we hope, have said the creed as part of their "Family Meals" or "Family Faith Breaks."

During these times, we have read these lines from the creed:

I believe in the holy catholic church,
the communion of saints.

These words may have seemed strange to some persons when they first professed them. Take a few moments and consider what this statement means to *you*. Record your thoughts below:

Families who are having their first encounter with the creed through the FaithHome experience may have some uncertainty about what it means to say that they believe in a "holy" church. They also may be totally bewildered by the references in the creed to "catholic" or "saints." This week we will work at finding our way beyond the uncertainty of these and other confusing images.

HOLY—CATHOLIC—COMMUNION OF SAINTS

HOLY — sacred, not secular or ordinary, belonging to God.

We say that the church is holy because it belongs in a special way to God and participates in God's sacred quality.

CATHOLIC — universal, encompassing everything.

When we use the word *catholic* (with a lower-case "c") to describe the church, we are talking about the whole church that is spread throughout all the world. The word *Catholic* (with a capital "C") refers specifically to the Roman Catholic Church, which at one time (before splits with the Orthodox and Protestant churches) was considered to be the one and only church throughout the entire world and was therefore described as "universal."

COMMUNION OF SAINTS — the gathering together and living in the presence of God of all believers in Christ who have by him been saved.

While Protestant Christians do not put a lot of emphasis on the saints, such as Saint Paul or Saint Teresa or others, we do affirm that all those who believe in Christ and seek to do God's will participate in God's holiness and are therefore sanctified by God. They are saints in that God has made them holy. The word *communion* means that in eternity, God gathers them together.

When Did the Church Begin?

When did the church begin? Many congregations throughout the world celebrate the birthday of the church on Pentecost Sunday, which is usually in late May or early June. The event of Pentecost is described in Acts 2. Take a moment and read that chapter in your Bible.

What insights can you draw from your reading? Make notes below:

Like our own birthdays, the first one of which is celebrated about twenty-one months after our conception, the Christian church began long before its birth date was marked at Pentecost! There can be no mistake: God caused the church to come into being. It was by the action of God's Holy Spirit that Pentecost happened. It was by the action of God that the formative events of the church occurred prior to Pentecost.

The Church Continues

The risen Christ commissioned the disciples to continue his mission in the world, proclaiming the good news of God's salvation. On the Day of Pentecost, Peter preached the good news to those assembled. People responded immediately to Peter's invitation to "repent, and be baptized every one of you in the name of Jesus Christ so that your sins may be forgiven; and you will receive the gift of the Holy Spirit" (Acts 2:38). As the story reminds us, "Day by day the Lord added to their number those who were being saved" (Acts 2:47).

Before we focus on the challenge of the church to be a worshiping, servant body of Christ (Weeks 6 and 7), it is vitally important to focus on the church's call to be a learning community. As in all things, we cannot give to others what we do not already have. For example, Jesus taught the disciples for three years before he left them physically. Throughout the three years, of course, the disciples had moments of service—service that they performed and then reflected on while Jesus was still with them. Jesus taught in many ways, including what we might call the action/reflection method.

To empower Christians fully to be "in the world to change the world," the church must be a learning community. The earliest believers knew the importance of instruction:

> **And these words which I command you this day shall be upon your heart; and you shall teach them diligently to your children, and shall talk of them when you sit in your house, and when you walk by the way, and when you lie down, and when you rise.**
>
> (Deuteronomy 6:6-7 RSV)

> **Do not forget the things your eyes have seen, nor let them slip from your heart all the days of your life; rather, tell them to your children and to your children's children.**
>
> (Deuteronomy 4:9 JB)

Jewish tradition made the family the locus of much of what was taught about faith. Each time a Jew entered the door of a home, a mezuzah—a small container attached to the door frame and containing the ancient words of the Shema—was touched. The Law was debated openly in the home, in the marketplace, and in the synagogue. The Law affected every aspect of Jewish home life, from dietary codes to worship. Even the pots a Jewish family used for cooking were affected by the Law. The Law was important because it enabled a Jew to live within the parameters of the covenant with God.

Consider for a moment how you learned to be a Christian. Who taught you about God? How did he or she teach you?

In what ways have you "told your children and your children's children"? Why?

What were your reasons for agreeing to lead FaithHome?

Knowledge of Scripture, stories of the faith, insights into the nature and validity of prayer, appreciation for the rudiments of worship, heightened awareness of sacramental living (see Week 9)—each of these and more is indispensable to the forming of Christian identity. We are a unique people, a people of a unique and very beautiful story. Discovering that story and exploring our role within that story is a sacred task.

A family may find it interesting to research their family tree. If their search leads to a deeper understanding of a genetic trait or brings awareness of genuine health risks, the search may become more than simply "interesting"; it may become life saving.

Similarly, the journey of forming a Christian identity may begin with a curiosity about one's past, a casual desire to know more. It may lead—and, we hope, will lead—to a life-changing, life-saving ending.

Educators of the Faith

What is the role of the family in the formation of Christian identity? What is the role of the church? In her book *Family, the Forming Center*, Marjorie Thompson maintains that family life is critical in the process of faith formation of children. She writes,

Christian spiritual formation requires conscious choice and a responsive awareness to the presence of the risen Lord in all life. I believe that families of committed Christian faith are privileged places of intentional formation in Christ—that, indeed, such families are the *primary* locus of faith formation for children and constitute a significant context for continued adult spiritual growth as well. I use the term *primary* both in the sense of *first* and of *principal.* . . . Children learn what they live.[3]

The goal of the FaithHome experience, therefore, is to empower Christian families with the ability and blessing to be primary nurturers and educators of the faith. In a sense, our approach is intended to allow families to experience in a fresh and exciting way the church as a learning, serving, and worshiping community. Leaders of FaithHome groups are significant in the process, but the process extends beyond the walls of a building and the gathering of all participants. Consequently, most of the time spent during the experience does not happen at the church. However much we might enjoy and benefit from meeting with others, the primary focus of the FaithHome experience is to involve individual Christian families in the practice of Christian "habits" and in the process of spiritual growth—to help them become a "laboratory for soul work."[4]

Consider what this might mean to you as a FaithHome leader. If you consider family life as a "laboratory for soul work," what is your role in that process?

Historically, the church has believed that religious nurture and education is the primary task of the home, supplemented by the rich resources of the church. Christian education in the church is vitally important; yet brief exposures at such gatherings as vacation church school, Sunday school, and confirmation class can never supplant the daily education a child receives in the home. Thus, the important questions become

—In what ways do Christian churches enable parents engaged in the task of spiritual formation?

—Are there training courses offered?
—Are there other supportive measures provided?
—Or do we communicate that the church is the primary—or, in some cases, the only—adequate provider of Christian education?

Families must be serious about providing Christian nurture and witness in the home, supported and assisted by the teaching opportunities of the church. Likewise, the church must be serious about providing families instruction, resources, and assistance for this important task. To borrow terms used by Marjorie Thompson, the "communal church" must equip the "domestic church" (the family) to be the primary educator of the faith. How can this happen in *your* congregation?

 ## LEADER'S WEEKLY SESSION GUIDE

Week 5: We Are a Learning Church

Objectives:

By the end of the session, children and adults will have

—talked together about how the church is people who believe in God and follow Jesus;
—learned about the early church;
—worshiped God through song and prayer.

 ## Materials Needed:

For Full Group: FaithHome video, video player and monitor, family banners, construction paper, scissors, crayons and markers, fish patterns (page 68), fabric glue, Christ candle, matches, cassette tape player, FaithHome tape

For Adults: copies for each participant of the Apostles' Creed (page 25, or use copies from previous weeks), newsprint, markers, tape, writing paper, pencils or pens, *Family Guides*

For Children: signing motions for the Apostles' Creed (page 24), Bibles, cassette tape player, FaithHome tape, large piece of felt for banner (see Activity 1), fabric paints, glue, scissors, washable felt-tip markers, wet wipes, 9" x 12" felt squares in a variety of colors, fish patterns (page 68), posterboard, foam meat trays, colored sand, craft sticks or paintbrushes, pencils, index cards, crayons or markers, copies of "Find the Missing Letters" (page 69) for the younger children, copies of "Church Crossword Puzzle" (page 70) for the older children

Welcome (3 minutes)

Welcome the group and thank them for being here for this fifth session of FaithHome. Ask one person from each family to share one thing the family enjoyed from their "Family Faith Breaks" or "Family Meals" during the past week.

Video Segment (10 minutes)

Introduce the video segment by saying something like this:

This week we will be talking about the church as a place for learning. Let's see what our friends on the video have to say. As you watch, think about how you would answer the questions. We will talk about that briefly after viewing the segment.

After playing the video segment, allow a few minutes for discussion (see page 11 for a list of questions to encourage discussion).

Group Activity (15 minutes)

This week each family will add a fish, representing followers of Jesus, to their family banner. On each table, place family banners, construction paper, fish patterns (note: cut out *without* ICHTHUS acrostic in center), fabric glue, markers, and scissors. Ask each family to work together to cut a fish out of construction paper and decorate it by drawing pictures or writing words describing things they have been taught at church. Encourage the families to talk about things they have learned and are learning at church and people who have taught them at church. Allow 15 minutes for the families to complete their fish and glue them to their family banners. Tell the participants that they will be sharing something about their fish during the closing time.

Adult Session (40-45 minutes)

(1) Repeat one or more of the questions from the video segment and allow the adults briefly to share their ideas.

—What comes to mind when you hear the word *church*?
—What does the church teach us?
—What is the ideal church?
—What would the world be like without the church?

OR

Invite them to talk about their experiences at home during the previous week.   (5 minutes)

(2) Hand out copies of the Apostles' Creed (page 25; use the same copies from previous weeks, if you like). Ask the group to read all the way through the creed and then reread the statements beginning, "I believe in . . . the holy catholic church." Invite each participant to share briefly what the church means to him or her.   (5 minutes)

(3) Divide the participants into groups of four. Ask each group to compile two lists, writing down the first thoughts that come to mind: (1) words and terms they associate with the church and (2) questions they think their children might have about the church. Come back together as a group and write on newsprint the questions the groups listed.   (5 minutes)

(4) Say to the group:

*What do you most remember about the "Background Basics" that you read in your **Family Guide** related to the church? I'd like to include points that had real meaning for you, questions that occurred to you as you read this material, or stories from your life or the lives of your children that you thought of as you read the material.*

Record on newsprint any questions that you may address together.   (2-5 minutes)

(5) Summarize the "Leader's Background Material" for Week 5, being sure to include the following points:

—Church is people, not a place or building.
—The words used for *church* in Hebrew, Greek, and Latin mean "called" or "called out."
—The church began at Pentecost.
—We use the word *holy* to indicate that the church is of God.
—We use the word *catholic* to show that the church is universal—not one denomination or sect.

—We use the term *communion of saints* to indicate that those who have gone before and those who come after are all teachers and learners together in the faith—the church.

—Just as Jesus, whom we follow, was a teacher, so also the church is called to teach and to learn.

—In the Jewish tradition, the locus of learning was the home. We as Christians also carry that tradition.

—What happens in the home is critical in the process of faith formation of children.
(10 minutes)

(6) Go back to the group's questions listed earlier and briefly answer any that have not been addressed. Invite responses from the group. When answering, try to move the group to reflection on what they think and feel the questions of their children will be related to the church (as a people, not a building).
(5 minutes)

(7) Now look at the group's list of questions that children might ask. Read each question; then ask for suggestions from the group about how to answer or discuss this question with children.   (10 minutes)

Children's Session (40-45 minutes)

Opening Circle (5-10 minutes)

Invite the children to sit with you in a circle. Play a name game. Show the children how to do a clapping rhythm by patting your knees with your hands two times, then clapping your hands together two times. The first time through, say:

My name is (your name).

to the clapping rhythm. The second time, call the name of a child in the group. Help the child whose name you have called to repeat the pattern, saying his or her name the first time and the name of another child the second time. Continue until each child has clapped his or her name and someone else's.

Ask the children:

What did you think about the video we watched?

Take a few statements from the group. Add statements of your own to help the children reflect on what they saw.

Show the children the activities that they will be doing.

Activity One: Art Center (10-12 minutes)

Footprint Banner

For Older Children: You will need a large piece of felt for a banner. Write at the top "We Are the Church," using a felt-tip marker. Provide 9" x 12" squares of felt in a variety of colors. Ask each child to choose the color of felt he or she likes. Pair the children and ask them to trace each other's foot onto a felt square using a washable felt-tip marker. (Have wet wipes on hand for the children to clean the marker off their feet.) Then instruct the children to cut out their footprints, write their names on them with fabric paints, and decorate them any way they wish. Let them attach their decorated footprints to the large banner!

For Younger Children: Young children will enjoy taking off their shoes and socks and having an adult or older child help them to make their very own footprints. After the "helpers" have cut out the footprints and have written the children's names on them, let the young children decorate them with washable felt-tip markers.

Activity Two: Discovery Center (5-8 minutes)

Learn About the Early Church

Provide copies of the fish with ICHTHUS printed in acrostic fashion (page 68). Remind the children that during Week 2, they learned in one of their "Family Faith Breaks" that ICHTHUS (the Greek word for fish) was a symbol for followers of Jesus. (Children will be proud and excited that they already know this information!) Briefly review how in the early days of the church, it was not always safe to admit that you were a Christian. The early Christians used the fish as a secret sign. When they met another person they did not know, they would trace half of a fish in the sand with a foot or stick. If the other person was a Christian, that person would complete the fish. If the other person was not a Christian, he or she would think the person was simply moving his or her foot in the sand. Ask the children if any of their families have been using the fish symbol as a greeting during the FaithHome experience.

For All Children: Make sand drawings using colored sand, posterboard, and glue. In advance, trace the fish pattern (page 68) onto posterboard and cut out a fish for each child. Let the children use paintbrushes or craft sticks to spread a thick layer of glue over their fish. Then they can sprinkle colored sand onto the glue to cover their fish. (You might want to cover the table or area with newspaper to make cleanup easier!)

For Younger Children: An optional activity for younger children is sand tracing. Provide several foam meat trays in which you have poured a layer of sand. Ask two older children to show the younger children how to trace a fish in the sand. Then let all the children have a turn tracing fish in the sand!

Activity Three: Study Center (5 minutes)

For All Children: Distribute Bibles to the older children. Have an older child read Deuteronomy 6:4-9 aloud. Then help the children begin to commit to memory Deuteronomy 6:4-5 by reciting the verse in rhythm together. Give each child an index card; also give the older children pencils. Ask each child to name one person at home or at church who has helped him or her to learn about God. The older children may write these names on their index cards. A "helper" will need to assist the younger children. Tell the children to bring these cards with them to the closing circle.

Distribute copies of the "Church Crossword Puzzle" (page 70) to the older children. If time permits, allow the children to work as partners to solve the puzzle. Or, ask the children to work on the puzzle at home.

Distribute copies of "Find the Missing Letters" (page 69) to the younger children. If time permits, help them to complete it and let them color the fish with crayons or markers. Or, send it home with the children and tell them to ask a family member to help them complete it.

Closing Circle (10 minutes)

Call all the children together in a circle. Let each child share one thing he or she has learned or done. Let each child say the name on his or her index card. After each child says a name, lead the children in saying together, "Thank you, God, for people who help us learn about you."

Using the poster on page 24, lead the children in signing the Apostles' Creed. Concentrate on the motions while you say the words. By now many will know this by memory. Do not be concerned if some still can do only the motions or only the words.

Teach the children the song "We Are the Church" and the motions (see pages 118-119). Tell the children they will help to lead their parents in the motions in a few minutes. End with a spoken prayer of thanks for this learning time together.

Closing Time (15 minutes)

(1) As the children and adults come together, ask the adults to go with their children back to the tables where they worked on their fish. Invite each family to show their fish to the group and tell about some of the things they have learned through church and through important people in their lives.

(2) After every family has had a chance to speak, ask the group to enter with you into a time of prayer. Light the Christ candle; then dim the lights. Pray, asking for God's guidance for each family present and for strength to continue in the commitment of study, discussion, reflection, and service. (After the prayer, turn the lights back on.)

(3) Say together the Apostle's Creed, letting the children help to lead the group in the motions they are learning.

(4) End by having the children sing along with the FaithHome tape to teach their parents the song, with motions, "We Are the Church."

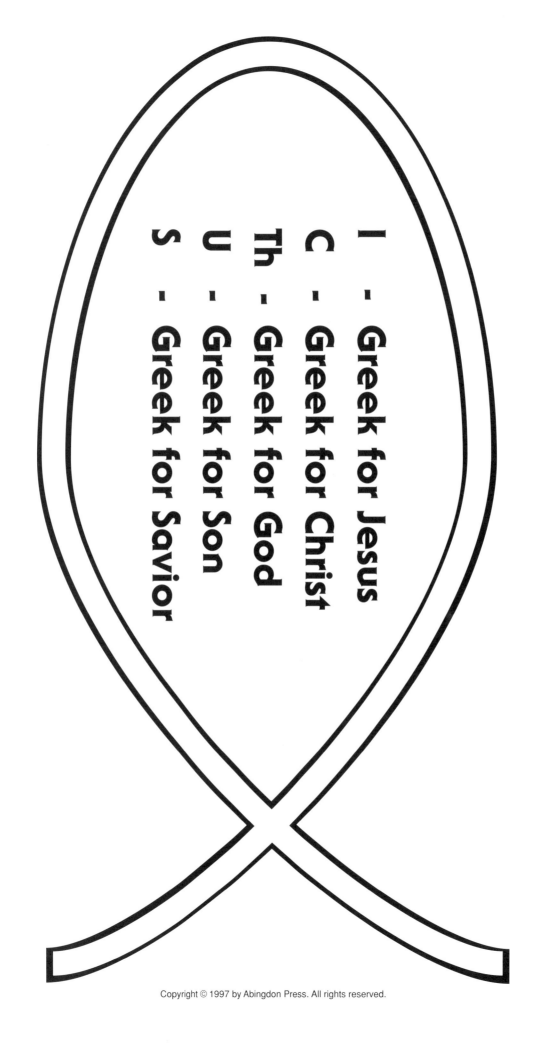

I - Greek for Jesus
C - Greek for Christ
Th - Greek for God
U - Greek for Son
S - Greek for Savior

Find the Missing Letters

There are some letters missing from these words.
Look at the number under the blank space; then find the missing letter
 that matches the number on this sheet.
When you have found all the missing letters, color the fish.

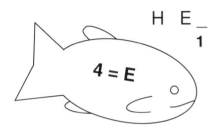

H E _ R, O I S R A E _: THE LOR_
      1   2   3

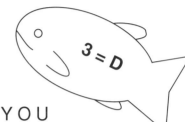

IS OUR GOD,

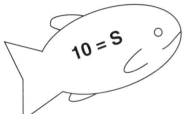

TH_ LORD ALONE. YOU
  4

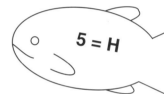

S_ALL LOVE THE
 5

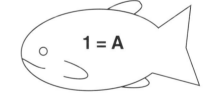

LORD _OUR GOD WITH ALL
     6

YOUR HEAR_,
         7

AND WITH ALL YOUR SO_L,
                   8

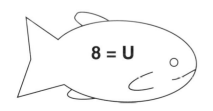

AND _ITH ALL YOUR
   9

_TRENGTH.
10

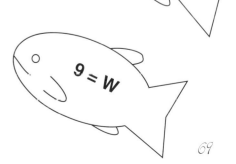

(Deuteronomy 6:4-5, NRSV)

4 = E
3 = D
10 = S
5 = H
2 = L
1 = A
6 = Y
7 = T
8 = U
9 = W

Church Crossword Puzzle

Read Acts 2 in your Bible.
Use this word bank to complete the crossword puzzle below.

Pentecost, Acts, Flames, Pray, Peter, People, Tongues, Fish

Across

1. We call this the birthday of the church.
2. This man preached the sermon at Pentecost.
3. At Pentecost, followers saw the Holy Spirit as _____ of fire.
7. A symbol of the early church.

Down

1. The church is not a building; the church is _____.
4. This book of the Bible contains the account of Pentecost.
5. The followers of Jesus had gathered in the Upper Room at Pentecost to _____.
6. The people at Pentecost spoke in different _____ so that others understood them.

We Are a Worshiping Church

What do we want our children to learn about the worship of God? However we respond to this question, there is one truth we can count on: Children will learn far more from their *experience* of worship than from any words we might use to describe proper worship to them. A recent event in one congregation proves the validity of the axiom.

It was a little thing, really—yet not so little. The congregation had come to that point in the worship service when the sacrament of Holy Communion would be celebrated. The parents of the five-year-old child had talked with her about Communion. She understood that Communion was a special kind of meal that we share with Jesus. During this Communion meal, a morsel of bread and the tiny cup of grape juice helped people remember how much Jesus loves them. Jesus, the child remembered her parents saying, invites everyone to share this meal with him. The parents had coached the child about what to expect when this particular congregation celebrated Communion: Worshipers passed trays of small squares of bread and the small cups of grape juice down the length of each pew. Seated an arm's length away from her parents, the little girl waited patiently, yet expectantly, to receive the trays.

For whatever reason, however, the usher was not with the same program! Purposefully reaching over the child, the usher passed the Communion elements beyond reach. It was a small action, probably intended to save a preschooler the embarrassment of dropping a tray. Or perhaps the usher decided on his own that the child was too young to participate in Holy Communion. Tears quickly welled up in the child's eyes. With reddened face, the child tucked her head, literally burying the tears deep within the palms of her hands. "I didn't get any!" she murmured.

Children learn what they live. Children learn what they experience. They learn more from what we do than from what we say.

Last week we explored the church as a learning community. This week we will explore the church as a worshiping community. As we do, keep in mind these critical issues:

—In what ways does the church enable persons of various ages to enter into the intimacy of Christian worship?
—Are there ways in which, perhaps unintentionally or unconsciously, we deny children full participation in worship?
—How might a new emphasis on Christian worship within the family as the "domestic church" (see Week 5) enrich worship within the "communal church"?

What was the community of faith declaring to one of its children in overlooking her desire to receive the bread and the cup? On a basic level, that preschooler had grasped at least a significant portion of the meaning of Holy Communion: She was supposed to be welcome at that small, strange meal. Jesus loved her and invited her. She knew that the special meal was one way in which her church family remembered Jesus—and she wanted to participate in the "lived message" of his life, death, and resurrection. On another level, she knew that most families do not turn away members who are hungry. From her viewpoint, however, she had been denied a place at that meal—turned away "hungry."

An adult—now a pastor—talked about why he is a Christian today: "I am a Christian today because going to church with my parents was one of the most natural things in the world. We were active in almost every aspect of congregational life. The adults around me made me feel at home in the church. I still feel like the church is my home."

 ## LEADER BACKGROUND MATERIAL

Why Worship?

A mother remembers a heightened sense of vulnerability at the arrival of a baby. She says, "Those first few nights, I hired a nurse so that I could get some sleep. I put three closed doors between myself and the baby. In the middle of the night, I would awake instantly when she cried. I thought about the prayer: 'Lord, hear our cry!' Before I didn't believe that God hears cries. But God is supposed to be our parent, and parents, I discovered, have incredibly good ears."[1]

The Scriptures speak of God as a great, powerful Presence who, remarkably, hears the cries of the human family. The psalmist pleads,

Hear, O LORD, and be gracious to me!
O LORD, be my helper!

(Psalm 30:10)

Then immediately the psalmist moves to praise God, who had heard the cries of a single individual:

You have turned my mourning into dancing;
you have taken off my sackcloth
and clothed me with joy,
so that my soul may praise you and not be
silent.

(Psalm 30:11-12)

We *need* to worship. The biblical commandment to observe the sabbath day in order to keep it holy is tied to the human need to worship God. Worship carves out a time and a place that is different from the harsh business of "making a living." Worship enables us to experience what it means to stop in the middle of life and just "be."

Our culture places a high priority on "doing." We tend to view our worth in terms of what we accomplish or earn. Money becomes a way of keeping score or determining how "good" we are. The idea of not performing, not accomplishing, not succeeding, is alien and difficult for many persons.

When we shift our perspective away from "doing" to "being," however, we often are able to glimpse a deeper meaning in life. Life is not intended for human beings to "rack up" one accomplishment after another. The "chief end" of human beings does not involve "doing" so much as "being" beloved creatures of the Creator. The Westminster Catechism reflects the true purpose of life when it declares, "The chief end of man [humanity] is to glorify God." In other words, our purpose is to engage throughout our lives in meaningful reflection about God— worshiping the One who "hears our cries."

So, what actually happens when we worship? When we worship God, we

—honor God, who is the Creator and Sustainer of all life;
—seek to be in God's presence, to get closer to this God who loves us so amazingly and so powerfully;
—find our lives recreated as we observe the holiness of time and place that takes us out of the world that drains our being;
—discover that God participates in and enlarges

that something within us—that soul, that spirit—that God created in us in God's own image.

Worship Is Adoration

Pastors, Christian educators, and others within the church are frequently asked their opinions about the propriety of children in worship. Often the question is phrased, "Children can't really understand and appreciate everything that goes on during a worship service, can they?" We might ask the same question about many—perhaps even most—adults. Even if we do not ask the question, many of us have the faulty assumption that worship is meaningful only if it is fully understood.

In fact, worship at its best involves an experience of awe in the encounter with that which we cannot understand, comprehend, or even fully appreciate. Worship is more than feeling good while singing old, familiar hymns; more than getting goose bumps hearing an especially beautiful choir anthem; more than gaining intellectual stimulation from well-turned phrases in the preacher's sermon. Of course, such things take place, and our worship is likely enriched as a result. Yet, worship is more about our coming into the presence of One who loves us and our attempt to reflect as much love back as we are humanly able. This is something children can do, too.

Worship at its best has a simplicity and innocence about it. Wherever worship occurs, we find ourselves drawn closer to God; and we end up adoring God.

Back in the 1970s, John Lennon of the Beatles created a momentary stir with his comment, "We're more popular than Jesus Christ!" On one level, Lennon's comment was blasphemous; on another level, it is quite instructive.

Think about the way that fans of a music or sports superstar act. Fans may stand in lines for hours and pay even hundreds of dollars for the privilege of spending a couple of hours witnessing the feats of a Michael Jordan or a Bruce Springsteen. Fans cheer, applaud, and work themselves into a frenzy on occasion. Some find themselves obsessed with the superstar, seeking to imitate the superstar in various ways. They adore the superstar. In a sense, they are worshiping.

Translate that kind of adoration to our worship of God, which involves adoring God at least as much as a fan adores a music or sports superstar! Children are as capable of worship as are adults. If anything, children are more spontaneous and readily authentic in their giving of love and adoration.

Jesus recognized this aspect of children when he scolded his disciples for attempting to prevent children from coming to him: "Let the little children come to me; do not stop them; for it is to such as these that the kingdom of God belongs. Truly I tell you, whoever does not receive the kingdom of God as a little child will never enter it" (Mark 10:14-15).

Many adults, parents among them, become uncomfortable when children squirm, fuss, and even misbehave (according to some assumptions about proper behavior during worship) in the pew during congregational worship. Many churches provide for "children's church" or an extended session of study in another part of the church building during all or part of the worship service so that children will not disrupt the adult experience of worship. Other children may occupy the worship service in less challenging ways, drawing pictures or sitting in stifled boredom. To be sure, there are exceptions to this grim picture—where children are meaningfully empowered to worship. But in the usual scheme of things, such exceptions are rarities.

The amazing thing may be that children who encounter worship as a time to draw pictures or as a time of stifled boredom actually come into a sanctuary as adults! Perhaps, instead of worrying over the behavior of children as they sit in the pew or fretting over how to keep them occupied, we should ponder whether our children are being meaningfully drawn into the awesome presence of God during the worship time. If they are not, something may be quite wrong with the way we are worshiping!

Think back to a recent Sunday morning. Reflect on these questions:

—Were children welcome in the sanctuary during worship? If so, how were they made to feel welcome? If not, how were they made to feel unwelcome?
—What were children doing during worship?
—How do you think the children experienced worship on that occasion?

Worship as Service

Most congregations commonly call the time on Sunday mornings and on other occasions when they gather in the sanctuary for worship "the worship service." What kind of act of serving goes on in worship? Who is being served and for what purposes?

Sometimes worship service attenders act as though they are the ones being served. They do not feel as if they have worshiped unless they come away feeling somehow fulfilled, or at least entertained.

Sometimes worship service attenders do enter into worship with a sense that they are somehow serving God with their worship. Biblically, this is a more appropriate attitude for worship. Among the burnt offerings and sacrifices the ancient Hebrews offered up on God's altar were those that were simply intended to please God. Many references appear in the Bible stating that God found certain kinds of burnt offerings pleasing in their smell. The point here is not that God prefers certain fragrances to others; the point is that we worship in order to please God. And the Bible also tells us that we please God best when we do God's will.

Worship helps to attune us to what God's will is for us. We hear the Word of God read and preached to us. The hymns, creeds, and prayers reinforce the directions in which God wills for us to move. Time and space are separated out of the ordinary so that we may better receive God's Spirit and hear what God would tell us.

God's will usually has something to do with moving out into the world and serving others. In Micah 6, God speaks through the prophet Micah to tell those who would worship God that instead of physically bowing before God and offering God tremendous burnt offerings, God prefers that people do nothing other than

**to do justice, and to love kindness,
and to walk humbly with your God.**

(Micah 6:8)

Helping Children Learn to Worship

Most traditional worship services might not be the best place to help children learn how to worship God. Think about how alien the experience of worship may be to most children. Most of the music is from "before their time." A special "church vocabulary" is used by the worship leaders: *liturgist, lectionary, anthem.* Whatever "action" there might be takes place in the front of the church and may be difficult for a small person to see easily. Though more and more churches are beginning to offer more worship alternatives, including celebratory or "contemporary" services, comparatively few churches use any dramatic, audiovisual, or interactive techniques that might prove effective to children, who are so familiar with television and electronic media.

Despite such difficulties, family worship can become a rich occasion to teach children the essentials of Christian worship and provide a place for children to experience and practice those essentials. In so doing, the "domestic church" becomes the primary educator about Christian worship.

Many of the traditional elements of congregational worship can find their counterparts within family worship: calling of the people from the ordinary world into worship, prayers, praise through song and other means, the reading and pondering of Scripture, and blessing as the people return to the ordinary world. Teaching of appropriate respect for the holy can easily begin in the home. Greater "hands on" participation of children in the different facets of worship can take place. Besides the worship suggestions offered throughout the FaithHome resources, many hymnals and prayer books offer daily prayer or daily "office" forms that may prove useful to families wanting help in establishing a family worship routine. Numerous other resources are available in many church libraries and Christian bookstores.

Understanding the Sacraments: God's Grace at Work

In order better to understand what worship is about, it is helpful to understand the meaning of the sacraments. Traditionally, Protestant Christians have equated the sacraments with two specific acts: baptism and Holy Communion, sometimes called by different names—the Lord's Supper, the Last Supper, the Eucharist, to name a few. (Roman Catholics enlarge the number of sacraments to include five other acts: confirmation, ordination, marriage, acts of penance, and sacrament of the sick—formerly called "extreme unction.") When we participate in the sacraments, we experience anew "God's grace at work" in our lives and in our midst.

Baptism

Various faith traditions within Christianity have different understandings about baptism. Some traditions practice infant baptism. Others practice only believer's baptism. Some congregations require candidates to be immersed; others allow for candidates to choose the most meaningful form of baptism for them. Despite divergent opinions, however, there are some common understandings. Baptism is the sign of God's seeking and saving grace. Whether it is the baptism of an infant or the baptism of an adult, the primary focus of baptism is the same. The focus is on what God is doing, not merely on the intent of those being baptized.

In an age of "how to" manuals and "do it yourself" philosophies, we are prone to appropriate sacramental occasions for the expression of our own agenda. Many would like to glide by Paul's declaration, "While we were still weak" (Romans 5:6), Christ died for us. Yet, it is when we are willing to be utterly dependent upon God's grace that God is "able to accomplish abundantly far more than all we can ask or imagine" (Ephesians 3:20). Baptism declares that God's seeking and saving love knows no limits.

Holy Communion

Holy Communion is the sign of God's sacrificing and sustaining love. As in baptism, the focus in Holy Communion is on God's work and not on our own agenda. Holy Communion is the sign of God's prior work of grace as well as of God's present work of grace. While the sacrament of Holy Communion includes "remembrance" of Jesus' self-giving through death, it is a serious mistake to limit Holy Communion to a "memory meal" or a memorial to the acts of Jesus. The Greek word for "remembrance," *anamnesis*, literally means "experiencing anew." In other words, Holy Communion is an experiencing anew of God's sacrificing and sustaining love through Jesus Christ.

The present power of God's sustaining grace and the awesome gift of sacrificial love are known in the symbols of bread and juice. We gather as Christ's family around the table to eat the food that nourishes us into life abundant and unto life eternal. Christ presides at the table. It is his table! He serves us the food we need to be faithful as a missional community. We eat—not to satisfy some private, warped craving for Christ, but to be nourished for faithfulness. We confess our sins and leave them in the cleansing, transforming grace of the Lord—not so that we can feel better, but so that we can live better and minister more justly to a world in need.

Whether it is the water of baptism or the bread and cup of Holy Communion, sacraments use the ordinary, common elements of life to convey extraordinary truth. The sacraments prevent the church from spiritualizing the faith through the use of common elements. It is in the "stuff" of our lives that God's Holy Spirit seeks to work. It is in ordinary moments and experiences that we bear witness to the transforming grace of God. It is in the midst of our humanity that we encounter the living God and therein seek to live the creed as faithful deed.

 ## LEADER'S WEEKLY SESSION GUIDE

Week 6: We Are a Worshiping Church

Objectives:

By the end of the session, children and adults will have

—discovered that worship is important for the church;
—learned how we worship God in church;
—learned why we have baptism and Holy Communion;
—worshiped God with song, prayer, and study.

 ## Materials Needed:

For Full Group: FaithHome video, video player and monitor, family banners, construction paper, scissors, markers, butterfly patterns (page 79), glue, fabric glue, glitter or sequins, Christ candle, matches, cassette tape player, FaithHome tape

For Adults: hymnals, newsprint, marker, tape, church worship bulletins, *Family Guides,* a copy of your church's budget for each family

For Children: signing motions for the Apostles' Creed (page 24); Bibles; cassette tape player and FaithHome tape; index cards; crayons and markers; scissors; glue; air-drying clay or play dough; pictures of Communion symbols: chalices, patens, bread, or grapes; pictures from church materials or photographs of persons being baptized; watercolors; paintbrushes; paper; several containers of water; worship table with the following objects: cross, offering plate, candles, Bible, hymnal; worship bulletins; copies of Psalm 100 (page 80); hymnal for each child

Welcome (3 minutes)

Welcome the group and thank them for being here for this sixth session of FaithHome. Ask one person from each family to share one thing they enjoyed from their "Family Faith Breaks" or "Family Meals" during the past week.

Video Segment (10 minutes)

Introduce the video segment by saying something like this:

This week we will be talking about the church as a place for worship. Let's see what our friends on the video have to say. As you watch, think about how you would answer the questions. We will talk about that briefly after viewing the segment.

After playing the video segment, allow a few minutes for discussion (see page 11 for a list of questions to encourage discussion).

Group Activity (15 minutes)

This week each family will add a butterfly, representing the re-creation of our lives through worship, to their family banner. On each table, place family banners, construction paper, butterfly patterns (page 79), glue, fabric glue, glitter or sequins, markers, and scissors. Ask each family to cut a butterfly out of construction paper and decorate it with markers and glitter or sequins (sprinkle over a thin layer of glue). Encourage the families to talk together about worship services at their church— what they enjoy, what they do not, and why—as they work. Allow 15 minutes for the families to complete their butterflies and attach them to their family banners. Tell them they will be showing their butterflies and sharing a learning about worship or a favorite family worship memory during the closing time.

Adult Session (40-45 minutes)

(1) Repeat one or more of the questions from the video segment and allow the group briefly to share their ideas.

—What do you enjoy most about worship?
—What is your favorite memory of worship?

—How can your family worship God at home?

OR

Invite them to talk about their experiences at home during the previous week.   (5 minutes)

(2) Ask each individual to think of a hymn or song of the church that has deep meaning for him or her. (Distribute hymnals, if you like.) Then invite persons to explain why this hymn or song is meaningful to them. (5 minutes)

(3) Ask the group:

Why do we sing the songs of faith?

Take comments from the group, listing these on newsprint. Remind the group that music and singing make up one element of worship. Then ask them to cite other aspects of corporate worship, quickly listing these on newsprint. (You may want to distribute copies of a worship bulletin.)   (5 minutes)

(4) Say to the group:

What do you most remember about the "Background Basics" that you read in your Family Guide related to worship and the sacraments of baptism and Holy Communion? I'd like to include points that had real meaning for you, questions that occurred to you as you read this material, or stories from your life or the lives of your children that you thought of as you read the material.

Record on newsprint any questions that you may address together. (2-5 minutes)

(5) Summarize the "Leader's Background Material" for Week 6, being sure to include the following points:

—We worship to glorify God.
—We worship to be involved in meaningful reflection about God.
—Worship is prayer, praise through music and song, reading and pondering Scripture, responding to Scripture through offerings, receiving blessings to carry us in daily life. (**Note:** *At this point, distribute copies of a weekly church bulletin from your church and talk about where you see the above elements of worship in the actual worship service(s) in your congregation. Also distribute copies of your church's budget and tell the*

group that they will be using this during their "Family Faith Break" on Day 3 of this week.)
—Corporate worship provides a setting in which we as Christians feed on the Word of God so that we can go into the world to feed others.
—Family worship teaches children the essentials of Christian worship and provides a place for children to experience and practice those essentials.
—Baptism is the sign of God's seeking and saving grace. (Review your church's practices of baptism.)
—Communion is the sign of God's sacrificing and sustaining love. (Recall together how your church practices Communion.) (10 minutes)

(6) Go back to the group's questions listed earlier and briefly answer any that have not been addressed. Invite responses from the group. When answering, try to move the group to reflection on what they think and feel their children's questions will be about worship, baptism, and Holy Communion. (5 minutes)

(7) Invite the group to share questions their children have asked about worship, baptism, or Holy Communion—or questions they think their children might ask. Ask for suggestions from the group about how to answer or discuss each question with children. (10 minutes)

Children's Session (40-45 minutes)

Note: *More activities are provided for this session than can be completed in 45 minutes. You may want to omit one activity or make adjustments as necessary to shorten the session. Although 45 minutes is the recommended time span for this part of the weekly experience, you may find it beneficial to exceed this time limit on occasion.*

Opening Circle (5-10 minutes)

Invite the children to sit with you in a circle. Play a scramble game. In advance, prepare index cards for the children, writing each of one of the following words or word groups on *two* index cards: cross, candle, Bible, hymnal, offering plate, altar, water, bread, juice, baptismal font or pool, bulletin. If there are younger children in your group, draw or glue pictures of the object on the two cards as well. Give one card to every child, making sure that there is a match for every card. Ask the children to look at their cards and remember what is on them. Say:

I am going to call the name of an object written/shown on two of the cards in our group. When you hear your object called, get up, shake hands with the other person who has the same object as you, and change places. If I say, "worship scramble," then everyone has to get up, shake hands with a friend, and sit down in a new place.

Continue until every child has heard his or her word. Tell the children that all the words you have called out are objects or things that are used in worship services at church. The children will be learning more about these things during this session.

Ask the children:

What did you think about the video we watched?

Take a few statements from the group. Add statements of your own to help the children reflect on what they saw.

Show the children the activities that they will be doing.

Activity One: Art Center (10 minutes)

Note: *You may divide the children into two groups and have each group do one activity, or let the children choose which activity they would like to do. If you plan to have all the children do both activities, you will need to allow more time in your schedule.*

Holy Communion

For Older Children: Talk with the children about your church's ritual of the Lord's Supper or Holy Communion and what happens when a person takes Communion. Then give the children air-drying clay or play dough and tell them to form it into symbols for Communion: chalices, patens, bread, or grapes. Have pictures of these symbols on hand for reference.

For Younger Children: Younger children will enjoy playing with the dough or clay and making loaves of bread, Communion wafers, or grapes. Let them enjoy creating without worrying about what their creations look like!

Baptism

For All Children: Post pictures from church materials of persons being baptized, or use photographs taken by persons in your church. Talk with the children about how people are baptized in your church.

Provide watercolors, paintbrushes, and paper; ask each child to paint a symbol of baptism. Provide water in various containers and encourage the children to pour the water from one container to another. Make a list together of all the ways we use water. Encourage the children to share their ideas about why we use water for baptism.

Activity Two: Discovery Center (10 minutes)

Learning About Worship

For Older Children: Give each child a worship bulletin from your church. Ask the children to read through the bulletin. Every time they see something in the bulletin that means we are to listen, ask them to underline this in green. Every time they see something we are to sing, ask them to underline this in red. Every time they see where we are to pray, ask them to underline this in blue. Tell the children that when we worship, we **PRAY** to God, **SING** praises to God, and **LISTEN** to God's Word through the Bible and the words of others.

Place the following objects on a worship table: cross, offering plate, candle, Bible, hymnal. Show each object to the children, asking them to guess why we use that object in worship. Explain that we use candles to help us remember God is with us in worship, and we take that light from worship into the world to help others know God. We use the Bible to help us know God's message to those who lived before us and God's message to us. We use the offering plate to give gifts of money to the church to carry out God's work. We use the cross to remind us of Jesus. We use the hymnal for singing praise to God.

For Younger Children: Take the children into the sanctuary. Let them play "I spy" looking for crosses, offering plates, Bibles, hymnals, and candles. Talk about how we use each of these objects in worship.

Activity Three: "Study" Center (10 minutes)

For Older Children: Distribute Bibles. Ask each child to find and read Psalm 100. Hand out copies of Psalm 100 (page 80); then help the children begin to commit the verse to memory by reciting it in rhythm together. The children may color the border with crayons or markers, if they like.

For Younger Children: Give each child a copy of Psalm 100 (page 80). Read the psalm aloud for the children, asking them to repeat the words after you. Let the children color the border with crayons or markers.

Closing Circle (10-15 minutes)

Call all the children together in a circle. Let each child share one thing he or she has learned or done. Ask them to show their decorated copies of Psalm 100. Say the psalm together in rhythm, letting the younger children repeat each line. Tell the children this psalm reminds us that we are to worship God; that we are to come together in places of worship to be with others who worship God; and that God is with us, just as God was with people during Bible times.

Using the poster on page 24, lead the children in signing the Apostles' Creed. Concentrate on the motions while you say the words. By now many will know this creed by memory. Do not be concerned if some still can do only the motions or only the words.

Give each child a hymnal. Have a brief time of singing together, helping the children locate a couple of songs in the hymnbook—such as "This Is the Day," "I'm Goin' a Sing When the Spirit Says Sing," "Praise God, from Whom All Blessings Flow," "Glory Be to the Father," or others that may be in your hymnal. If time allows, play the song "We Are

Faith Families," singing along with the FaithHome tape. End with a spoken prayer of thanks for this learning time together.

Closing Time (15 Minutes)

(1) As the children and adults come together, ask the adults to go with their children back to the tables where they worked on their butterflies. Invite each family to show their butterfly to the group and to share one of their learnings about worship, or they may prefer to share a favorite family worship memory.

(2) After every family has had a chance to speak, ask the group to enter with you into a time of prayer. Light the Christ candle; then dim the lights. Pray, asking for God's guidance for each family present and for strength to continue in the commitment of study, discussion, reflection, and service. (After the prayer, turn the lights back on.)

(3) Say together the Apostles' Creed, letting the children help to lead the group in the motions they are learning.

(4) Sing "This Is the Day," "I'm Goin' a Sing When the Spirit Says Sing," or another favorite from your hymnal or from the FaithHome tape. End with the song "We Are Faith Families" (page 117), singing along with the FaithHome tape.

79

Psalm 100

1 MAKE A JOYFUL NOISE TO THE LORD,
   ALL THE EARTH.

2 WORSHIP THE LORD WITH GLADNESS;
   COME INTO HIS PRESENCE WITH SINGING.

3 KNOW THAT THE LORD IS GOD.
   IT IS HE THAT MADE US, AND WE ARE HIS;
   WE ARE HIS PEOPLE, AND THE SHEEP
      OF HIS PASTURE.

4 ENTER HIS GATES WITH THANKSGIVING,
   AND HIS COURTS WITH PRAISE.
   GIVE THANKS TO HIM, BLESS HIS NAME.

5 FOR THE LORD IS GOOD;
   HIS STEADFAST LOVE ENDURES FOREVER,
   AND HIS FAITHFULNESS TO ALL
      GENERATIONS.   (NRSV)

We Are a Witnessing and Serving Church

A number of years ago, a family helped to build a Habitat for Humanity house. Both parents had been very involved in the project—organizing other volunteers; donating money for the project; and providing some of the "sweat labor" as painters, landscapers, and so forth. Finally, the house neared completion. On Friday evening before the dedication on Sunday, the family gathered on their deck to eat together. When everyone had eaten, there was a lull in the conversation. Everyone was tired! Only the baby had the energy to talk, making "babble" sounds amidst the fireflies and coming dusk.

After a few moments, the conversation turned to how nice it was that they could enjoy another meal on the deck. The weather was lovely for an October evening; flowers continued to bloom and were fragrant near the deck. The parents contentedly sipped coffee and thought about another family—a Habitat family—who would soon enjoy a new home. Suddenly, the seven-year-old child got up from the table. Returning with his bank, he pulled out about ten dollars of savings. "It isn't fair!" he shouted. "That family will be moving into a house without pretty flowers and a yard of dirt and grass seed. Let's buy as many flowers tomorrow morning as we can and plant them in their yard."

The next morning, Habitat fever infected even the nursery owner. Hearing the story of a little boy giving his savings for a family to beautify their home, she willingly sold several mum plants at a fraction of their value. As the family took the mums to the car, she shouted after them, "I'll bring by some shrubs this afternoon. And tell the Habitat committee that they can count on us donating flowers and shrubs for every house they put up in this county!"

At that time, the little boy did not have the ability to think concretely, *I am part of a witnessing and serving church*. He only knew that giving of what he had and serving in ways he could were important. Since this first endeavor, he and his family have participated in the building of three additional Habitat homes—and each time, mums have been quietly purchased on the eve of the house dedication and planted in a roughly landscaped yard.

An unusual occurrence? No! Christian families throughout the ages have demonstrated love and concern for others. These demonstrations have ranged from such acts as building a home for a marginalized family and hiding Jews from the Nazis to sending a card to a grieving family or caring for the children of a harried young parent for an afternoon. The actions themselves are less important than the impetus behind them.

Consider some of the ways in which you have tried to show love or concern for others. What motivates you? Write your thoughts below:

transformation I could never do that!

This week we will focus on the church as a witnessing and serving community. We begin by exploring what we mean by Kingdom living.

 ## LEADER'S BACKGROUND MATERIAL

Kingdom Living

Throughout his ministry, Jesus demonstrated the contours of the kingdom of God. As the Gospel accounts describe Jesus' teachings, he did not so much define what the kingdom of God is as describe what the Kingdom—and life within the Kingdom—is like. Jesus' own life and lifestyle can be seen to fit within that description.

As Jesus described it in the parables he told, the kingdom of God is like

- —a mustard seed that grows from the smallest of all seeds to the greatest of shrubs (Matthew 13:31-32);
- —yeast that leavens a small quantity of flour to make a hundred loaves of bread (Matthew 13:33);
- —a treasure hidden in a field that is worth selling all one has in order to buy the land in which it is hidden (Matthew 13:44);
- —a fine pearl worth purchasing at any price (Matthew 13:45-46);
- —a fishing net that catches every kind of fish in the sea so that once it is brought ashore, the good and the bad fish need to be separated (Matthew 13:47-50);
- —and more.

We also learn from Jesus' parables certain truths, such as that in God's kingdom

- —both small and great debts are forgiven (Luke 7:41-43);
- —a true neighbor is the one who shows mercy to a person in need, not necessarily the one belonging to the same nation, race, or neighborhood (Luke 10:29-37);
- —persistence in prayer is a virtue (Luke 11:5-8);
- —the accumulation of material wealth is foolish (Luke 12:16-21);
- —great joy is expressed when one who is lost is found (Luke 15:1-32);
- —God's gifts are meant to be invested and used, not hoarded (Luke 19:11-27);
- —and more.

Jesus was the demonstration of the very kingdom he announced. Throughout his life and ministry there was wholeness of life, fulfillment of spirit, and reconciliation in relationships. He lived life joyfully in obedience to God and in service to others. People experienced the new life of the Kingdom as they responded to the preaching, teaching, healing touch, and caring ministry of Jesus. Remember Zacchaeus? Conversation with Jesus over a meal transformed his life, as he encountered One who loved him.

Luke describes well the reality of the Kingdom: "Once Jesus was asked by the Pharisees when the kingdom of God was coming, and he answered, 'The kingdom of God is not coming with things that can be observed; nor will they say, "Look, here it is!" or "There it is!" For in fact, the kingdom of God is among you' " (Luke 17:20-21).

Christians sometimes in error pray for strength to build the kingdom of God. Some of our hymns talk about "growing" the Kingdom, and some of our teachers have encouraged students to help God's kingdom come on earth. While we may grow in our understanding of the Kingdom or even empower ministries that demonstrate the Kingdom, the kingdom of God has already been perfectly demonstrated in and through Jesus. Christians are merely given the responsibility of offering ourselves in ways that help to make known the Kingdom to the hurting, the helpless, and the marginalized.

Scripture describes our role this way:

Come, you that are blessed by my Father, inherit the kingdom prepared for you from the foundation of the world; for I was hungry and you gave me food, I was thirsty and you gave me something to drink, I was a stranger and you welcomed me, I was naked and you gave me clothing, I was sick and you took care of me, I was in prison and you visited me.

(Matthew 17:34-36)

Jesus continued in startling fashion: "Truly I tell you, just as you did it to one of the least of these who are members of my family, you did it to me" (Matthew 17:40). And for those who do not live like Kingdom people, Jesus spoke the word of accountability and judgment: "Truly I tell you, just as you did not do it to one of the least of these, you did not do it to me. And these will go away into eternal punishment, but the righteous into eternal life" (Matthew 17:45-46).

Take a few moments to reflect on these questions. Write your responses in the space provided:

—In what ways are you involved in proclaiming the Kingdom in your community?

—In what ways is your congregation involved in proclaiming the Kingdom?

—In what ways does your participation and leadership in the FaithHome experience help to proclaim Kingdom living?

Kingdom Living Involves Selfless Giving

Kingdom living has a particular focus on the poor, who are viewed, not as objects of mission, but as members of Jesus' family with whom we have a relationship, a relationship that includes responsibility. Unfortunately, however, amidst the affluence of North America, it is not uncommon to hear Christians disparage the poor. It comes as a shock to success-oriented achievers to discover that the poor may have a stronger possibility of "success" in being Kingdom participants than do the affluent. All this may move us to ask, "Does God give guidance for the use of our resources?"

Listen to one guiding principle:

For those who want to save their life will lose it, and those who lose their life for my sake, and for the sake of the gospel, will save it. For what will it profit them to gain the whole world and forfeit their life? Indeed, what can they give in return for their life? Those who are ashamed of me and my words in this adulterous and sinful generation, of them the Son of Man will also be ashamed when he comes in the glory of his Father with the holy angels. (Mark 8:35-38)

Did you know that the average giving to all charitable causes by American Christian families ranges between two percent and three percent of family income? The biblical guideline for the giving of our income is a tithe—ten percent. Christians sometimes wonder whether the tithe is figured on one's "take home pay" or "gross income." Perhaps the best answer is that God is not interested in legalism. God wants us joyfully to share our resources—ourselves—on behalf of God's mission among the human family. The apostle Paul said it this way: "Each of you must give as you have made up your mind, not reluctantly or under compulsion, for God loves a cheerful giver" (2 Corinthians 9:7).

The use of our money is intimately connected with whether we turn a creedal witness to our belief in Jesus into a demonstration of the Kingdom he announced and lived. In fact, Jesus puts his finger on the crux of our relationship to money in a most uncomfortable statement: "For where your treasure is, there your heart will be also" (Matthew 6:21).

A man once gave a multimillion-dollar gift to a charitable institution. Shortly afterward, he lost his wealth. A friend questioned him, "Don't you wish you had that big gift back?" The man responded quickly: "Under no circumstances! That gift is all I really do have!"

Believers know that each of us has been given a gift in Jesus Christ. Therefore, Kingdom living involves all of who we are—including our wealth. It requires that we use what we have been given, in particular, on behalf of the poor and marginalized.

Children, even at a very young age, can be encouraged to give of personal possessions or money. In one family, family members gather each Saturday night to place individual amounts in an envelope for their church offering. "Big" decisions involving income are discussed at a family meeting. In these ways, the children have learned from early ages that decisions made today impact other decisions tomorrow. They also have learned to think about how their decisions impact the environment and one another.

Not long ago, one of the children in this family became very interested in owning athletic shoes that "light up." A children's magazine arrived days after he purchased his new shoes. When he discovered that some states had banned the shoes because the chemicals used in the shoes were harmful to the environment when they disintegrated, he insisted on taking them back to the store. An interesting conversation followed between the store manager and that child!

When we teach our children to be selfless givers, we teach them how to live in God's kingdom.

Kingdom Living Involves Servanthood

To the consternation of some of his followers, Jesus taught and lived that Kingdom living involves servanthood. Jesus said, "I am among you as one who serves" (Luke 22:27), as he took a basin and towel and washed the tired, dusty feet of his companions. Then he commanded his companions to imitate his example (see John 13:13-17).

Serving God by serving others is the lifestyle of a Christian. Power, privilege, and prestige are not the marks of a successful Christian or of a successful church. The Kingdom question for every congregation is, Is this a servant church? Do its members share the joyful vision of offering themselves in ministries with the poor, the marginalized, the victims of discrimination, those of lost dreams, the imprisoned, those in bondage to addiction, those suffering from the ills of the world? Servanthood is rarely glamorous! It is, however, godly.

The life of Jesus was living proof that healing the hurts of others demonstrates Kingdom living. He did not engage in healing to acquire a following; manipulation was not his manner. Neither did he share his power to demonstrate that he had it. On the contrary, Jesus used the power given to him by God in order to serve humankind faithfully.

What does it mean for you to say, "I believe what Jesus preached, taught, and lived"?

Released for the Care of the World

In our final phase of the FaithHome experience, we will explore how living sacramentally helps Christian families become "sacred shelters" of love and stability. While some might suggest that the primary purpose of "sacred shelters" is to protect the family from the evils of the world, such an idea is far from accurate. In fact, our focus this week suggests that the real purpose of a "sacred shelter" is to "release its members for the pastoral care of the world."[1] How? Christians are best released for the pastoral care of the world—involving outreach, mission, stewardship, and the like—as a result of the "spiritual nurture and training of the home."[2] The FaithHome experience, then, helps to equip families for the holy mission of Christians in the world.

 ## LEADER'S WEEKLY SESSION GUIDE

Week 7: We Are a Witnessing and Serving Church

Objectives:

By the end of the session, children and adults will have

—explored the meaning of "Kingdom living";
—experienced ways to be of service to others;
—worshiped God through song and prayer.

 ## Materials Needed:

For Full Group: FaithHome video, video player and monitor, family banners, construction paper, scissors, markers, candle patterns (page 89), fabric glue, Christ candle, matches, cassette tape player, FaithHome tape

For Adults: newsprint, markers, tape, *Family Guides*

For Children: signing motions for the Apostles' Creed (page 24, or use copies from previous weeks), instant-developing camera and film, construction paper or 9" x 12" posterboard for each child, glue, crayons and markers, index cards and magazines (see Activity 2), scissors, Bibles, writing paper and pencils, cassette tape player and cassette tapes (see Activity 3), biblical costumes (such as bathrobes, see Activity 3), copies of "Promises to Keep" (page 90)

Welcome (3 minutes)

Welcome the group and thank them for being here for this seventh session of FaithHome. Ask one person from each family to share one thing they enjoyed from their "Family Faith Breaks" or "Family Meals" during the past week.

Video Segment (10 minutes)

Introduce the video segment by saying something like this:
This week we will be talking about the church as a place for witness and service. Let's see what our friends on the video have to say. As you watch, think about how you would answer the questions. We will talk about that briefly after viewing the segment.

After playing the video segment, allow a few minutes for discussion (see page 11 for a list of questions to encourage discussion).

Group Activity (15 minutes)

This week each family will add a candle to their family banner, representing our responsibility to share the light of Christ with others. On each table place family banners, construction paper, candle patterns (page 89), markers, scissors, and fabric glue. Ask each family to cut a candle out of construction paper and use colorful markers to write on it words or phrases describing ways they can serve others. Encourage the families to talk about ways Christians witness and serve by how they act and what they do. Allow 15 minutes for the families to complete their candles and glue them on their family banners. Tell participants they will be sharing something about their candles during the closing time.

Adult Session (40-45 minutes)

(1) Repeat one or more of the questions from the video segment and allow the adults briefly to share their ideas.

—What does it mean to be a witness for Jesus Christ?
—How would you complete this sentence: The kingdom of God is . . .
—What are some ways you and your family can help others?

—What's the hardest thing to teach children about giving?

OR

Invite them to talk about their experiences at home during the previous week. (5 minutes)

(2) On one sheet of newsprint, write the word "Witness"; on another, write the word "Serve." Ask the group to suggest words and phrases that explain what it means to witness and what it means to serve. List these on the appropriate sheets. Now ask the group to share questions they have about what it means to be a serving and witnessing church, writing them on another sheet of newsprint. Circle any that participants feel are also questions their children might ask. Ask what other questions children might have; add these to the list. (12 minutes)

(3) Summarize the "Leader's Background Material" for Week 7, being sure to include the following points:

—In the Bible, Jesus talks about the kingdom of God, giving us guidelines for living as Christians.
—Kingdom living is life lived in obedience to God and in service to others.
—Jesus compares the kingdom of God to many things. (You might ask volunteers in the group to look up the following Scripture passages and read them to the group: Matthew 13:31-32; Matthew 13:33; Matthew 13:44; Matthew 13:45; Matthew 13:47-50.)
—In God's kingdom, debts are forgiven, people respond to the needs of their neighbors, and wealth is shared so that no one goes without.
—Giving is a sign of Kingdom living.
—Healing the world's hurts is a sign of Kingdom living.
—What Jesus preached, taught, and did are God's words for how we are to think, talk, and act. (10 minutes)

(4) Go back to the group's questions listed earlier; briefly answer any that have not been addressed. Invite responses from the group. When answering, try to move the group to reflection on what they think and feel their children's questions will be about what it means to witness and serve. (5 minutes)

(5) Now look at the group's list of questions that children might ask. Read each question; then ask for suggestions from the group about how to answer or discuss this question with children. (10 minutes)

(6) Ask each adult to reflect quietly for a few minutes about how he or she can witness and serve as a parent (or caregiver). End with a brief prayer. (3 minutes)

Children's Session (40-45 minutes)

Opening Circle (5 minutes)

Invite the children to sit with you in a circle. Play a "popcorn" game. Tell the children you want them to think of ways we can show our love for others at home, at church, at school, or anywhere else we might be. Explain that you will begin, shouting your answer as you jump up like a kernel of popcorn. Tell them that they are to do as you do, shouting their own answers as they jump up. There is no "order" to follow; rather, the object is to see how quickly all the children can "pop" like popcorn! After all the children have shouted a response, have them sit down again.

Ask the children:

What did you think about the video we watched?

Take a few statements from the group. Add statements of your own to help the children reflect on what they saw.

Show the children the activities that they will be doing.

Activity One: Art Center (10 minutes)

I.D. Posters

For Older Children: Take a picture of each child, using an instant-developing camera. Ask each boy and girl to glue his or her picture to the center of a sheet of construction paper or to the center of a 9" x 12" posterboard. Have them print their names above their pictures and the words "is a child of God" below their pictures. Ask them to "frame" their pictures with drawings of things they like to do and ways they serve God at church and at home. Give some suggestions, such as contributing money to church or taking care of a younger brother or visiting lonely neighbors.

For Younger Children: After taking a picture of each child and attaching it to construction paper or posterboard, print the child's name above the picture and the words "is a child of God" below the picture. Then let the children decorate their posters as they wish. As they work, ask them to tell you some of the things they can do to serve God at church and at home. Write these on their posters for them.

Activity Two: Discovery Center (10 minutes)

Witness and Serve Coupon Books

For Older Children: Give each child four or five index cards. Ask the children to make "coupon cards" by writing on each card one thing they can do for someone else to show love and care for that person—as we have been taught to do by Jesus. You can list some suggestions on posterboard for the children to consider, such as,

—This coupon good for reading a Bible story.
—This coupon good for a hug.
—This coupon good for washing the dishes.
—This coupon good for cleaning up trash in the yard.
—This coupon good for a song to cheer you up.
—This coupon good for helping with the laundry.

Let them decorate their coupons by drawing borders or cutting and pasting pictures from magazines on them. Ask each child to think of someone to give each card to this week. Tell them to be sure to sign their names to the cards!

For Younger Children: Let the children draw or cut and paste pictures from magazines on one or two index cards, depicting something they can do to show love and concern for others. Ask an older child to help a younger child decide what to write below the pictures. For instance, "This coupon good for feeding the dog" might appear below a picture of a dog.

OR

Service and Witness Promises

For All Children: Make a copy of "Promises to Keep" (page 90) for each child. Ask the boys and girls to think about the three words on the sheet: TALK, PRAY, ACT. Now ask them to think about whom they might talk to about God, whom or what they might pray about, and what they might do in their family or

community to show God's love. Have the older children write their ideas on their papers; younger children can draw pictures or cut and paste pictures from magazines on their papers.

Activity Three: Study Center (10 minutes)

For Older Children: Distribute Bibles. Ask each child to find a partner and together read Luke 10:30-37. Now ask each pair to "rewrite" this story as if it happened in their community. Encourage them to think who might be the Samaritan in their community and who might be the priest (or pastor) in their community. They may want to think of themselves as the ones who were robbed and hurt. Instruct them to write their stories, record their stories on tape, or be ready to act out their stories for the rest of the group.

For Younger Children: Make an audio recording of the story of the good Samaritan in advance. Let the children listen to the taped story. Provide simple biblical costumes (bathrobes work well) and encourage the children to act out the story they have heard.

Closing Circle (10 minutes)

Call all the children together in a circle. Let each child share one thing he or she has learned or done. Ask two of the children who rewrote the parable of the good Samaritan to read their version of the story for the rest of the group. Talk together about ways the children can witness and serve at home and in their community. Explain that this is part of what it means to be a light in the world.

Using the poster on page 24, lead the children in signing the Apostles' Creed. Concentrate on the motions while you say the words. By now many will know this activity by memory. Do not be concerned if some still can do only the motions or only the words.

Listen to "I Have Decided (to Follow Jesus)" and then sing along with the FaithHome tape.

Closing Time (15 minutes)

(1) As the children and adults come together, ask the adults to go with their children back to the

tables where they worked on their candles. Invite each family to show their candle to the group and share one of their learnings about what it means to be a follower of Jesus by witnessing and by serving others.

(2) After every family has had a chance to speak, ask the group to enter with you into a time of prayer. Light the Christ candle; then dim the lights. Pray, asking for God's guidance for each family present and for strength to continue the commitment of study, discussion, reflection, and service. (After the prayer, turn the lights back on.)

(3) Say together the Apostle's Creed, letting the children help to lead the group in the motions they are learning.

(4) End with the songs "Jesus Is Calling" and "We Are Faith Families," singing along with the FaithHome tape.

Promises to Keep

TALK

I promise to talk about God by

PRAY

I promise to pray about

ACT

I promise to act as a Christian at home by

I promise to act as a Christian in my community by

Signed _____   Date _____

Living with the Bible

In previous weeks we have learned that to recite the creeds of the church is to declare our loyalty and belief. This week we turn our focus to the Bible, which reveals the witness and work of God and helps to form the way we talk about faith and live life.

What does it mean to "live with the Bible"? What practical help and hope does the Bible offer for today's parents and families? These are some of the questions we will be exploring this week as we consider how God's story intersects with the stories of our lives.

 ## LEADER'S BACKGROUND MATERIAL

The Power of Story

"Remember when . . . ?" Any parent knows that children love stories, particularly stories that involve them or people they know. Parents often tell and retell stories about a child's birth, infancy, and young childhood. The stories must sound the same from one telling to another. Details, such as the season of the year or the color of the baby blanket, are important in the telling of these stories; they are reminders of rich history. "Where did we live when I arrived?" "When you first saw me, what did I look like?" "What color was our house?" "What was my first word?" And the big one: "When you and Daddy first saw me, did you know then that you would love me?"

Of course, it helps when the storyteller also is willing to provide a lap for young listeners to sit upon. One particular three-year-old boy loved stories. He loved to curl up in the lap of a loved one and be told one story after another. One day, when his parents were very busy, he asked to sit in their laps and be told a story. They should have taken the time. They knew it then; they know it now. Admittedly, however, they were busy that day. And so, like many other busy parents, they said something like, "In an hour we will be through. Please play in your room or turn on the television and watch a program during that time." Crestfallen, the little boy turned away. Before leaving the room, however, he fired this shot: "But, Mama, TV doesn't have a lap!"

Stories—told with or without a lap—help us form our families. Stories help to form family distinctiveness and remind us of family history. The story bears within it both memory of ancient beginnings as well as future hopes and dreams. Stories have power!

One woman remembers being told as a child of the early days of her family as they settled on the prairies of eastern South Dakota and western Minnesota. The stories took on a life of their own as parents and grandparents, aunts and uncles, recounted tales they had been told of brush fires, economic depressions, poverty, and comfort. Older family members delighted in telling each tale. They wanted her to understand the kind of people from which she had come. It seemed to her then, and still does today, that she came from hardy stock—stubborn and courageous, not easily dismissed. And yet, the stories also spoke of kindness and warmth. There is a sense in which she has "lived into" that impression. The stories have helped to shape who she is—stubborn and not easily dismissed, with a tender interior. Family lore gave this woman a "window" into family expectations, goals, and dreams.

When Our Story Meets the Sacred

When that woman's family members and family friends entwined the telling of the Scriptures among the telling of family lore, there was a powerful, sacred connection made. The family was a unique clan deeply rooted in faith. The stubborn, warm family was sustained over and over again by the God to whom the Scriptures bore witness. When drought and depression ended a grandfather's farm in eastern South Dakota, moving the family to western Minnesota, offspring envisioned a trek not unlike that of Joseph's brothers from drought-stricken Palestine to Egypt. And when children and grandchildren learned of a particularly feisty grandmother who confronted an equally feisty county official, they could envision their link to Queen Esther confronting evil Haaman. Descendants could look across the room and see an antique rocker and remember that only the dearest or most practical of possessions were carried by wagon across the prairies. And the family could wonder about the possessions the Israelites took with them when they began the Exodus.

Marjorie Thompson clarifies the value in biblical identification when she writes,

One of the most critical functions of family storytelling is to help its members make connections between their personal stories and God's great story. . . . One of the beauties of scripture is that we can find ourselves in its stories in fresh ways throughout a lifetime. We may identify with different characters at various stages of life. We may also identify with the same character in different ways over time, discovering a new depth or unexpected trait in the biblical figure because of changed self-perception or life circumstance. If we approach scripture as a living word, we will find that it both embraces and expands our own experience.[1]

What stories can you remember from your childhood that held power for you? What stories helped form your understanding of your family or your place in it?

What stories were you told in childhood that helped you understand the good news of the Christian faith? Who told them?

For Christians, there is power in a particular story, the story of our faith. It is good news, encompassed in ancient lore, dramatic intrigue, mystery, and miracle. It is the story of a loving Creator God yearning for us. Marjorie Thompson writes movingly,

For Christians, one great story encompasses all other stories—the good news. Scripture tells the great story from beginning to end: from the creation of all that is, through the covenant promises made to Israel, to the fulfillment of those promises in Jesus, and on to the promised culmination of Jesus' risen life in the kingdom of God—a story that engages us to the core because the dynamics of human sin and divine faithfulness speak to our condition as truly now as they did when the stories of the Bible were first told.[2]

A Mirror and a Window

The story of our families has already been written. As surprising as that may seem, our hopes, dreams, and parenting challenges as well as our inner feelings and personal actions are all in the Bible. When we read the Bible, we find ourselves looking in a mirror—a rather unusual mirror. It shows us more than ourselves. The Bible mirrors God. We are shown God's care and love for us, for our families, and for all humankind.

The Bible has sometimes been called the "book of all books," for it is remarkably honest about the signs, struggles, saving acts, and second chances that affect our lives as parents and children. For example, in the Bible we are confronted by the blunt portrayal of family jealousy and favoritism (Jacob and Esau), youthful friendship (Jonathan and David), self-pity (Psalms and Lamentations), and erotic love (Song of Solomon). Parental pain and joy are real in the biblical stories of barrenness and pregnancy (Abraham and Sarah). The Bible empowers us to face our own faith and fears as parents. We learn of the anguish of Moses' mother in setting her child afloat in a reed basket and of a father's anguish in setting a son "afloat" to an even more fragile future called "coming of age"—and we intuitively know the pain of each person. In this way, the Bible "mirrors" many of the events of our lives or our feelings as we live.

The "mirror" of Scripture serves also as a "window" through which we can see a future destination. The "window" of Scripture points us toward a final destination by giving instructions, helpful hints, clues, or real-life examples from which we can learn to live abundantly. The Bible guides us in answering persistent questions parents often verbalize: "Am I being a good parent?" "What is the most important thing I can give my child?" "Is there a reason to have hope in the midst of some of our messes?" "Can I be the parent I want to be?" The Bible helps us answer these questions by giving us example after example of how persons have followed new directions toward new destinations.

THE BOOK OF BOOKS

When we think of a library, we naturally think of a collection of books. In fact, that is what the Bible is and what the word *Bible* means. The Greek word *biblia*, meaning "the books," has given rise to the word *Bible*. So, the Bible is a collection of books—sixty-six of them. In those Bibles that contain the Apocrypha—writing considered sacred but not included in the canon—the number of books may increase to seventy-three.

The word *canon* literally means "measuring rod." In Hebrew history and early Christian history, when many sacred writings were available to people of faith, it became important to establish the "officially designated" sacred writings, which were considered the standard for guiding the faith development of followers.

The Old Testament—as we know it—was canonized in the first century. The New Testament was canonized in the fourth century. While certainly every believer will have favorite passages or will find more help in some books than in others, traditionally the books of the canon have been considered "divinely inspired." As 2 Timothy 3:16-17 declares, "All scripture is inspired by God and is useful for teaching, for reproof, for correction, and for training in righteousness, so that everyone who belongs to God may be proficient, equipped for every good work."

Nourishment for the Family

Sharing the Bible together as a family resembles eating a meal together. Unless a member is very young or has an aversion to a particular kind of food, all family members usually eat the same food around the table. The Bible is a book that is a book for children, youth, and adults. We can be nourished all our lives from it. When we read the Bible, we participate in the lives of people who are searchers, strugglers, or even antagonists with respect to spiritual truth.

The act of sharing the Bible together sends a clear message about the importance of grounding one's life in God and in God's Word. This act of sharing is a statement about the priorities of parents and the family. If parents brush their teeth after every meal, for example, children soon learn that dental care is important. So it is with Bible reading. Children learn what they live! When children see parents cherishing the Scriptures, they witness a behavior they can come to understand as important.

What's more, when parents read the Bible devotionally, children see them differently. When parents read the Bible, pray, and allow their own vulnerability to be seen in the context of a spiritual framework, children see the importance of this approach to life.

When and where we read the Bible are not the critical considerations. That we, in fact, do read the Bible is what is important. The Bible may be read at any hour of the day—at home, at work, in the waiting rooms of hospitals or service centers, or when we commute to our jobs (if we're not driving, of course!)—as well as at some other designated location and time. Families who have not cultivated a time to share the Bible together should determine when and where they can do so.

In one family, Bible reading works best before bedtime. Even when one parent works late or attends a meeting, they can usually arrange to gather for a brief time before going to bed. Another family shares in prayer and a brief passage from the Bible at the end of the dinner meal. In the home of a single father, the family meets for a brief time before everyone leaves for work and school.

How does *your* family use the Scriptures at home?

What changes might be helpful to make that time more valuable?

Families who read the Bible together have made a commitment to "make connections between their personal stories and God's great story."[3] The connection is best made when families

—make and keep a commitment to read Bible passages or tell Bible stories together;
—cultivate a relaxed atmosphere around this spiritual discipline so that family members welcome rather than resent it;
—understand that young children will naturally move or be distracted during brief devotional periods and that these periods should take into consideration the needs of children;
—encourage both parents and children, as they are able, to participate as fully as possible in leadership.

God, a loving parent, is constantly seeking to nourish and renew a relationship with us. Regular personal and family Bible reading enables us to experience God's searching, welcoming love.

HELPING INDIVIDUALS AND FAMILIES CHOOSE A BIBLE

How can you help individuals and families in your FaithHome group choose the Bible translation that is right for them? It is important to understand and communicate that there are many adequate translations of the Scriptures. However, no one translation is error free, any more than the original Greek or Hebrew were absolutely correct renderings. Just as we invoke the leading of the Holy Spirit prior to reading the Bible, so translators have sought divine guidance in doing their work. Therefore, using more than one translation may be of benefit to most individuals and families.

Translation vs. Paraphrase

Many people ask if there is a difference between a translation of the Bible and a paraphrase of the Bible. The answer, of course, is "Yes!" It is important to help people understand those differences. A translation intentionally takes the original text, such as Greek, and renders it into its equivalent word meaning in another language, such as English. A paraphrase takes many more liberties to put the original text into another language. Paraphrases often illustrate the application of a text, as well as state its meaning. A paraphrase can be very helpful in understanding the meaning of a text. However, the reader should be aware that a paraphrase is not a translation. For this reason, a paraphrase is not adequate for serious Bible study.

When individuals or families are choosing a Bible, they should consider which translation and particular edition of that translation might be most helpful to them. For example, some Bibles have specific kinds of study helps, descriptions of each book, concordances for looking up particular texts, information on pertinent geography, or tables of weights and measurements common to the biblical period. Suggest that individuals consider their own needs and the needs of their families as they read a few familiar passages from several translations and compare the various study helps offered in each edition.

Bibles for Children

If a parent or caregiver needs help in choosing a Bible for a child, remind him or her to consider whether the reading level of a particular Bible is appropriate for the child. (Several Bible translations and the corresponding reading levels are listed below.) Though it is true that a child can always "grow" into a Bible, adults should consider how long the child will need to wait to begin to use the Bible by himself or herself.

Bible	Reading Level
New Revised Standard Version	8th grade
Living Bible	8th grade
Good News Bible: The Bible in Today's English Version	7th grade
New International Version	7th grade
The New Century Version	5th grade
King James Version	12th grade
New King James Version	8th grade
New American Standard	11th grade
Contemporary English Version	5th grade

Bible	Reading Level
The Children's Bible	young children

(Not a translation but a book of paraphrased Bible stories published by Golden Press in 1965)

A Complicated Decision?

The differences in reading level, the exactness of a translation, and the myriad of study helps available can make the choice of a Bible a complicated one. However, the relatively inexpensive cost of Bibles, the easy availability of them, and the variety of good translations and paraphrases make it possible—and even desirable—to own more than one Bible. In fact, most individuals and families will own and use many different Bibles as they mature in mind and spirit.

LEADER'S WEEKLY SESSION GUIDE

Week 8: Living with the Bible

Objectives:

By the end of the session, children and adults will have

—experienced ways we use the Bible;
—explored some different translations of Bible passages;
—worshiped God through song and prayer.

 ## Materials Needed:

For Full Group: FaithHome video, video player and monitor, family banners, construction paper, scissors, markers, Bible patterns (page 99), fabric glue, Christ candle, matches, cassette tape player, FaithHome tape

For Adults: several translations of the Bible, newsprint, markers, tape, writing paper, pencils or pens, *Family Guides*

For Children: signing motions for the Apostles' Creed (page 24, or use copies from previous weeks),

Bibles (including at least three different translations), self-hardening clay, rolling pins, toothpicks, Bible storybooks (see Activity 2), 2" x 3" pieces of posterboard (two for each child), 12-inch strips of ribbon (three for each child), glue, construction paper, crayons and markers, writing paper, pencils, copies of "Favorite Bible Verses" (page 100) for younger children, stapler, large posterboard, cassette tape player, FaithHome tape

Welcome (3 minutes)

Welcome the group and thank them for being here for this eighth session of FaithHome. Ask one person from each family to share one thing they enjoyed from their "Family Faith Breaks" or "Family Meals" during the past week.

Video Segment (10 minutes)

Introduce the video segment by saying something like this:

This week we will be talking about the Bible and what it has to say to us as growing Christians. Let's see what our friends on the video have to say. As you watch, think about how you would answer the questions. We will talk about that briefly after viewing the segment.

After playing the video segment, allow a few minutes for discussion (see page 11 for a list of questions to encourage discussion).

Group Activity (15 minutes)

This week each family will add a Bible to their family banner. On each table, place family banners, construction paper, Bible patterns (page 99), fabric glue, markers, and scissors. Ask each family to cut a Bible out of construction paper and "illustrate" it by writing Bible references (chapters and verses) for particular stories or verses they have enjoyed learning as a family. Allow 15 minutes for the families to complete their Bibles and glue them on their family banners. Tell participants they will be sharing something about their Bible during the closing time.

Adult Session (40-45 minutes)

(1) Repeat one or more of the questions from the

video segment and allow the adults briefly to share their ideas.

—What's your favorite Bible verse or story?
—Why is the Bible important?

OR

—Invite them to talk about their experiences at home during the previous week. (5 minutes)

(2) Write the following statements on newsprint:

In my opinion, the Bible is . . .

My favorite Bible story is . . . because . . .

A Bible verse that is important to me is . . .

A Bible that has special meaning for me is . . .

Give the participants writing paper and pencils or pens and instruct them to complete the statements as quickly as possible. (5 minutes)

(3) Divide the participants into groups of three or four and have them share and discuss their completed statements. Ask each group to note any comments or questions they would like to share with the larger group. (5-7 minutes)

(4) Summarize the "Leader's Background Material" for Week 8, being sure to include the following points:

—Bible stories help shape our lives and the lives of our children.
—We find ourselves in stories from the Scripture.
—The Bible mirrors God.
—The Bible empowers us to face our own faith and fears as parents.
—The Bible is a window giving us instruction, hints, clues, and examples for living faithfully.
—"All scripture is inspired by God and is useful for teaching, for reproof, for correction, and for training in righteousness, so that everyone who belongs to God may be proficient, equipped for every good work" (2 Timothy 3:16-17).
—Reading the Bible in front of children and with children helps them to build an appreciation for and dependence on the Bible.
—Regular personal and family Bible reading

enables us to experience God's searching, welcoming love.
—As adults, we find different translations and paraphrases helpful to our learning.
—As parents, we can help our children choose Bibles appropriate for them at different stages of their lives. (**Note:** *Here it would be good to use the chart on pages 94–95, explaining what makes each Bible helpful to adults and/or children. Show the group different translations/paraphrases and pass these around so that the group has a chance to read from several.*) (10 minutes)

(5) Ask at least four different readers, reading from four different translations, to read aloud Matthew 28:18-20. Lead the group in a discussion of why they enjoy a particular translation of the Bible. Then talk about which translations would be appropriate for their children. (10 minutes)

(6) Invite the group to share and respond to any unanswered questions. When answering, try to move the group to reflection on what they think and feel their children's questions about the Bible will be. (5 minutes)

(7) Ask each individual quietly to reflect on how he or she can begin or continue regular Bible reading and study with his/her children. (3 minutes)

Children's Session (40-45 minutes)

Opening Circle (5-8 minutes)

Invite the children to sit with you in a circle. Tell the children you are going to play the "gossip game." They are to remember what they hear and pass it on word-for-word to the next person. There are two rules: (1) They must whisper, and (2) they can repeat what they are passing on only one time. Begin with the child on your left and let the "gossip" go around the room, coming back to you. Ask the last child what he or she heard. Then ask the first child to repeat what you told him or her. Now tell the children the statement you started with. Say something like this:

Because we know we don't always remember what we've been told or what we've heard, people have learned that it is better to write down what we want to remember. That's what happened with our Bible. It began as stories people would tell to one another about God and God's works. Then they began writing this down so that what they knew of God and of Jesus wouldn't be forgotten or changed.

Ask the children:

What did you think about the video we watched?

Take a few statements from the group. Add statements of your own to help the children reflect on what they saw.

Show the children the activities that they will be doing.

Activity One: Art Center (5-10 minutes)
Bible Bookmarks

For Older Children: Each child will need two pieces of posterboard cut 2" x 3," three 12-inch ribbons, glue, and markers. Instruct each child to glue the ribbons side-by-side onto one piece of posterboard and then to glue the other piece of posterboard on top of the ribbons. Have each child write his or her name on the cardboard, along with a favorite Bible verse. The children can mark a special passage by sliding their bookmarks into their Bibles and allowing the ribbons to hang down.

For Younger Children: Help the children assemble their bookmarks. Rather than writing a Bible passage on their bookmarks, have them use crayons or markers to decorate their bookmarks however they wish.

OR
Bible Tablets

For All Children: Use self-hardening clay to make Bible tablets. Each child will need a small ball of clay. Tell the children to use rolling pins to flatten the clay and then use toothpicks to write a Bible verse or saying such as, "God is love" into the clay. (Younger children can make decorative scratchings in the clay.) Place the tablets where they can dry.

Activity Two: Discovery Center (10 minutes)
Explore Bible Translations

For Older Children: List the following Scripture references on a posterboard so that all the children can see them: Psalm 119:33; Psalm 119:105; Isaiah 40:31; Matthew 7:7; John 3:16; Ephesians 4:32. Have available three or four different translations of the Bible. Give each child a sheet of writing paper and a pencil. Ask the children to choose one of the verses

of Scripture listed on the posterboard, to look up that Scripture in three different translations, and to write the verse from each translation on their papers. Then have them circle the one they like best.

For Younger Children: Provide two or three different Bible storybooks that tell the same Bible story. Have an older child or an adult read each of the storybooks to the children. Then show the children where the story is found in a children's Bible. Let each child tell which storybook he or she likes best.

Activity Three: Study Center (10 minutes)
Bible Verse Booklets

For Older Children: Distribute Bibles. Use the same posterboard list of Bible verses used in Activity 2. Ask each child to find and read every Bible verse. Then give each child four or five sheets of writing paper and a pencil and ask him or her to write on each sheet a favorite Bible verse from those he or she has just read. Encourage children who have other favorite Bible verses to look up those verses and write them on other sheets of paper. Instruct the children to staple their papers between two sheets of construction paper to make booklets, writing "My Favorite Bible Verses" on the cover. Have the children sign and date their booklets.

For Younger Children: Give each child a copy of "Favorite Bible Verses" (page 100) and six sheets of writing paper. Have the children cut apart the verses and glue one verse to each sheet of writing paper. Have an older child or an adult help them staple their pages between two pieces of construction paper and write "My Bible Verse Booklet" on the cover. Be sure to write each child's name and the date on his or her booklet.

Closing Circle (5-7 minutes)

Call all the children together in a circle. Let each child share one thing he or she has learned or done. Invite the children to show their Bible verse booklets. Talk about how the children and other family members can use their booklets at home to memorize the verses.

Using the poster on page 24, lead the children in signing the Apostles' Creed. Concentrate on the motions while you say the words. By now many will know this creed by memory. Do not be concerned if some still can do only the motions or only the words.

Listen to "Wonderful Book of God's People" or "Teach Me Your Ways, O Lord"; then sing along with the FaithHome tape.

Closing Time (15 minutes)

(1) As the children and adults come together, ask the adults to go with their children back to the tables where they worked on their Bibles. Invite each family to show their Bible to the group and share one Bible story that they have enjoyed reading together.

(2) After every family has had a chance to speak, ask the group to enter with you into a time of prayer. Light the Christ candle; then dim the lights. Pray, asking for God's guidance for each family present and for strength to continue the commitment of study, discussion, reflection, and service. (After the prayer, turn the lights back on.)

(3) Say together the Apostles' Creed, letting the children help lead the group in the motions they are learning.

(4) End with the songs "Wonderful Book of God's People" or "Teach Me Your Ways, O Lord" and "We Are Faith Families," singing along with the FaithHome tape.

(5) Ask each family to bring their Christ candle from home to the final session of FaithHome next week. (**Note:** You might plan to have several extra Christ candles on hand in case some families forget to bring theirs.)

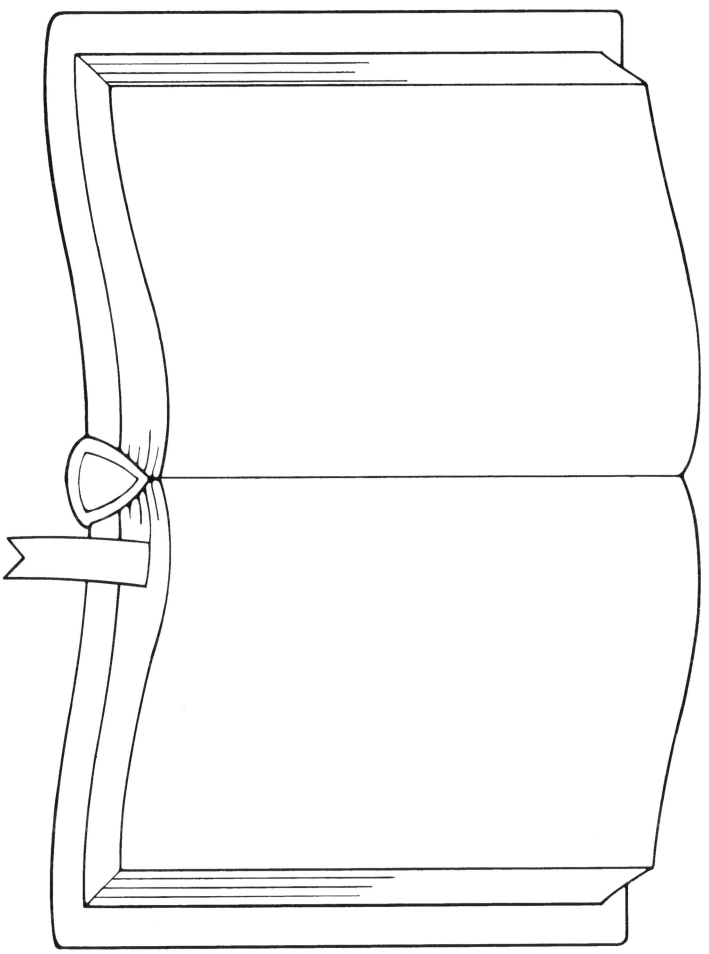

Favorite Bible Verses

"Ask, and it will be given you; search, and you will find;
knock, and the door will be opened for you."
(Matthew 7:7 NRSV)

"Truly I tell you, whoever does not receive
the kingdom of God as a little child will never enter it."
(Luke 18:17 NRSV)

"For God so loved the world that he gave his only Son,
so that everyone who believes in him may not perish
but may have eternal life."
(John 3:16 NRSV)

Jesus spoke to them, saying, "I am the light of the world.
Whoever follows me will never walk in darkness
but will have the light of life."
(John 8:12 NRSV)

"I give you a new commandment, that you love one another.
Just as I have loved you, you also should love one another."
(John 13:34 NRSV)

Be kind to one another, tenderhearted, forgiving
one another, as God in Christ has forgiven you.
(Ephesians 4:32 NRSV)

Living Sacramentally

Most adults don't think much about baths. We usually take showers to get clean, and that is the end of the matter. Children challenge that utilitarian perspective. For the parents of small children, baths have only a little bit to do with getting children clean and a lot to do with the actual process of giving a bath. It is an integral part of the cycle of the day. Parents speak not about a "bath" but about "bath time."[1]

So writes Nancy Fuchs, author, rabbi, wife, and mother of two, in her book on parenting as a spiritual journey. For Rabbi Fuchs, each day spent as a family evokes challenges, spiritual adventure, and transformed perspective. She reflects,

Living with small children was a crash course in all the themes I studied (throughout twelve years of academic settings beyond high school): love, grace, creation, revelation, forgiveness, law, suffering, power. Ten years later, it was clear that parenting was the most intensive seminar on spirituality around. I should not have been surprised. Deuteronomy says that wisdom "is not in heaven . . . neither is it across the sea. . . . It is very near to you."[2]

Is it possible to glean spiritual insight from such mundane, daily rituals as bathing? Can Christian families deepen spiritual wisdom as a result of the ordinary routines, events, and people near to them? What does it mean to live sacramentally? As we consider these questions, we turn our focus toward how families can continue the FaithHome experience and the Christian habits they have been practicing within their families during these nine weeks.

 ## LEADER'S BACKGROUND MATERIAL

Sacramental Living: Finding Meaning in Daily Events

A family watched in awe as a tiny warbler wove a nest in the center of a fern hanging on their front porch. They marveled at her insight! She had carefully chosen to make a home within ten feet of a bird feeder, at a home where the family usually uses the back door rather than the front door, and in the shade of a fern and a dogwood tree.

Day after day the family patiently watched as the mother bird laid her eggs, hatched and fed her fledglings, and finally urged them from the nest. Throughout the process, the family's two boys, ages five and eleven, asked questions. They marveled at the agility of a bird to sustain flight. They anxiously watched the mother as the nest and the fern were battered by wind and rain. They prayed when the mother finally kicked the young finches from the nest, "coaching" them to find shelter in a nearby tree. The opportunity to provide a "safe house" for a family of warblers was really an opportunity to witness the abundant care of a creator for the created. One day, the younger son put it all together: "Mama, does God care for us like that?"

Marjorie Thompson writes,

A simple lay monk, Brother Lawrence, made famous the phrase, "practicing the presence of God." He was speaking of a conscious awareness of God in the midst of washing dishes, preparing meals, and having conversations in the community that was his "family". . . . Family life is an arena in which most of us have natural occasion to "practice" God's presence—to learn the discipline of keeping our eyes open to the divine Reality shining through our most ordinary moments.[3]

That, Thompson says, is living sacramentally—intentionally exploring ways to claim and celebrate God's presence in our very midst. Families who live this way, she argues, become "sacred shelters." In these families, a framework of stability and love is intentionally constructed.[4] That is essentially what FaithHome is all about.

Throughout the FaithHome experience, participating families have been learning and practicing how to become "faith homes"—or sacred shelters—where all family members are continually learning and growing together in faith (belief), love, and Christian service. Ordinary "rituals" or routines that Christian families practice every day play a very important role in this growth process we call faith formation.

Ritual Makes Meaning

In the earliest days of the Christian movement, the church was strengthened through covenantal relationships—one Christian with another, often meeting in small groups in believers' homes—in which believers could pray, worship, have fellowship, commune together, and engage in meaningful service or witness. Baptism and Holy Communion (highlighted in Week 6) were two means of embracing ritual and sacrament.

Today, families are in desperate need of creating secure foundations. How? Just as the sacraments of the church make visible the grace of God through common substances of water, bread, and juice/wine, so also the ordinary routines and "rituals" of our lives—seen clearly with eyes open to the truths of God—become avenues for faith development. To borrow from Marjorie Thompson, "Part of our task . . . [is] 'to discover the spiritual disciplines inherent in the very structure and nature of family life,' and . . . 'to explore creative ways to incorporate time-honored practices into contemporary family life.' "[5]

What "time-honored practices" help your family celebrate God's presence?

Ritual makes meaning. Specifically, Christian ritual helps Christian believers find spiritual meaning.

A mother of two is frequently reminded, "We do it this way!" In her home she realizes that tradition, or ritual, helps to create arenas of comfort and security. When bath time follows supper and precedes quiet play or story time as the norm of the household, children begin to feel secure in the routine.

The parents of a four-year-old child were profoundly reminded of the meaning of ritual when they employed a sitter for a much-needed evening

away from home. They had briefed the sitter on the usual bedtime ritual. It was a simple routine: dinner, bath, story time, hugs, and prayer. However, a telephone call interrupted the latter part of the routine. Returning home, the parents found an upset boy and a harried sitter! "I missed you," sobbed the child. "He wasn't here!" Puzzled parents looked to the sitter for explanation. Why was the child so upset? And who was their son talking about? "Everything was fine," responded the sitter, "until I neglected to tuck him in bed and pray with him." Bedtime ritual in this family had always included prayer, followed by whispered reminders: "I love you and grandparents love you and, most of all, God loves you. And God will be with you all through the night." The simple words of a bedtime prayer provided a way for the boy to celebrate the presence of God in the midst of everyday life.

Christian families often find that living sacramentally helps them stay connected—to one another as well as to life-sustaining values. Marjorie Thompson reminds us,

Becoming conscious of God's spirit in the ordinary routines of our day and learning to respond takes time and practice. That is the significance of particular disciplines like family worship, ritual, and prayer. . . .

Children need to see that the spiritual life is significant to their parents at home as well as at the church. Otherwise the artificial dichotomy between faith and life that marks the modern church is reinforced and perpetuated. Children need to see their parents setting time aside for prayer, worship, reflection and open discussion about issues of faith: "Without modeling, children may not be inspired to give expression to their own spiritual lives."[6]

What particular spiritual disciplines have taken time and practice for you to find them meaningful?

Prayer: An Essential Ritual

Prayer has been a predominant theme throughout the FaithHome experience, for it is through prayer that we open ourselves to God's divine presence in our midst. Through prayer we draw close to the heart of God and to one another. Prayer

—declares our readiness for a relationship with God;
—expresses our confidence in the ways of God;
—testifies to our desire to share our life with God.

The earliest Christians bore witness to the importance of prayer. The New Testament instructs Christians to "devote yourselves to prayer, keeping alert in it with thanksgiving" (Colossians 4:2). Jesus invited his followers to approach God in the intimacy of a child's relationship to a parent.

Many adults question whether children can develop an appreciation for engaging all of life through prayer. The answer is "Yes!" How? As we have suggested, the ritual of prayer—particularly family prayer—is essential for faith formation and spiritual growth. Through regular family prayer, children learn the importance of prayer while gaining valuable experience in the practice of prayer. Through prayer we all learn to live sacramentally.

As your weekly FaithHome gatherings are ending, the experience of becoming "faith homes" is only beginning. Sacramental living, grounded in the habit of prayer, is the key that will enable families to continue the journey of discovery and growth in faith, love, and Christian service.

In what ways have you grown as a result of leading this FaithHome experience?

Week 9: Living Sacramentally

Objectives:

By the end of the session, children and adults will have

—participated in experiences of prayer;
—learned what it means to live sacramentally;
—considered how they can make prayer an important part of everyday life;
—worshiped God through song and prayer.

✂ Materials Needed:

For Full Group: FaithHome video, video player and monitor, family banners, construction paper, scissors, markers, praying hands patterns (page 107), fabric glue, Christ candle, each family's own Christ candle (have them bring these from home), matches, cassette tape player, FaithHome tape

For Adults: copies for each participant of the Apostles' Creed (page 25), newsprint, markers, tape, writing paper, pencils or pens, *Family Guides*

For Children: signing motions for the Apostles' Creed (page 24); lemons or apples (one for each child); air-drying clay or play dough; large, smooth rocks (see Activity 1); paint and paintbrushes; water and several containers; newspaper; crayons and markers; construction paper; index cards (6-8 for each child); scissors; yarn; hole punch; stickers or pictures cut from magazines (see Activity 1); Bibles; wide lengths of ribbon in assorted colors; glue; fabric paint or markers; clothes hangers; cassette tape player; prepared cassette tape (see Activity 2); FaithHome tape

Welcome (3 minutes)

Welcome the group and thank them for being here for the ninth and final session of FaithHome. Ask one person from each family to share one thing they enjoyed from their "Family Faith Breaks" or "Family Meals" during the past week.

Video Segment (10 minutes)

Introduce the video segment by saying something like this:

This week we will be talking about living sacramentally— what it means to live our faith day by day. Let's see what our friends on the video have to say. As you watch, think about how you would answer the questions. We will talk about that briefly after viewing the segment.

After playing the video segment, allow a few minutes for discussion (see page 11 for a list of questions to encourage discussion).

Group Activity (15 minutes)

This week each family will add praying hands to their family banner, symbolizing the importance of prayer to faith development and sacramental living. On each table, place family banners, construction paper, praying hands patterns (page 107), fabric glue, markers, and scissors. Ask each family to cut praying hands out of construction paper and write on the hands words or phrases that show some of their family's prayer concerns. Allow 15 minutes for the families to complete their praying hands and to glue them on their family banners. Tell participants they will be sharing one of their prayer concerns during the closing time.

Adult Session (40-45 minutes)

(1) Repeat one or more of the questions from the video segment and allow the adults briefly to share their ideas.

—How does your family love one another?
—What's your favorite family ritual?
—When does your family pray together?

OR

Invite the adults to talk about their experiences at home during the previous week. (5 minutes)

(2) Hand out a copy of the Apostles' Creed to each participant (page 25). Ask the group to read all the way through the creed, then to go back and underline words or phrases that could be used as a prayer for families and for the church. (5 minutes)

(3) Ask each person to find a partner and use the words they have underlined to write a prayer for families and for the church. (5 minutes)

(4) Write the word "Prayer" on a sheet of newsprint and post it in front of the group. Say to the participants:

What do you most remember about the "Background Basics" related to sacramental living and prayer? As I cover this topic, I'd like to include points that had real meaning for you, questions that occurred to you as you read the material, or stories from your life or the lives of your children that you thought of as you read the material.

Record on newsprint any questions that you may address together. (2-5 minutes)

(5) Summarize the "Leader's Background Material" for Week 9, being sure to include the following points:

—Daily rituals nurture us in faith. (Ask the group to suggest times in their family life, such as "bath time," that have become a ritual and a way of being together.)
—Practicing spiritual disciplines such as prayer in the home provides the framework for faith.
—We are called to look for God's presence in the routines of life.
—Children need to see parents involved in prayer, Bible study, and worship to believe such activities are valuable for them.
—Prayer is essential for faith development and sacramental living. *(Ask for some examples of favorite family prayers for mealtime, bedtime, or other times. Talk about what role these family prayers play in encouraging children to develop vital prayer lives of their own.)* (10 minutes)

(6) Go back to the group's list of questions and briefly answer any that have not been addressed. Invite responses from the group. When answering, try to move participants to reflection on what they think and feel their children's questions about sacramental living—seeing and celebrating God's presence in the ordinary routines of our daily lives— and prayer will be. (5 minutes)

(7) Now list on newsprint one or two questions that children might ask. Ask for suggestions from the group about how to answer or discuss these questions with children. (8 minutes)

(8) Read aloud the prayers written previously to close the session. (3 minutes)

Children's Session (40-45 minutes)

Opening Circle (5-8 minutes)

Invite the children to sit with you in a circle. Play the lemon game. (Note: Apples can be substituted for lemons if desired.) Give each child a lemon and ask him or her to study the lemon for a few minutes and then decide what makes the lemon special to him or her. Give some examples such as, "This lemon is special because it is perfectly yellow all over," or "This lemon is special because it is the first lemon I have ever held." After a few minutes, go around the room and have the children tell their names and why their lemons are special. Talk with the children about how we have learned to know one another during this study and how, just like these lemons, we are now special to one another.

Ask the children:

What did you think about the video we watched?

Take a few statements from the group. Add statements of your own to help the children reflect on what they saw.

Show the children the activities that they will be doing. Say:

As part of the FaithHome experience, you and your family have been learning about prayer and praying together. Today we will learn more about this important thing called prayer.

Activity One: Art Center (8 minutes)

Prayer Rocks

For Older Children: Let each child select a rock from those you have gathered. Tell the children that sometimes it is easier to remember to do something if we have an object to help us remember. Tell them that these rocks will be their prayer rocks. Every time they see their prayer rocks, they will be reminded to pray. Cover the tables with newspaper. Place bowls of water on the table along with paintbrushes and various colors of paint. Let the children paint their rocks with small pictures or words of things they want to remember to pray for.

For Younger Children: Allow the children to paint their prayer rocks however they like!

OR

Prayer Pockets

For older children: Give each child two pieces of construction paper. Instruct the children to cut one piece in half and then glue the half sheet to the full sheet by putting a thin line of glue around three edges, leaving one side open. Tell each child to write his or her name on the prayer pocket, along with the words "Prayer Reminders." After giving six to eight index cards to each child, ask the children to write one thing they can pray for on each card. Suggest such things as people who have no home, countries where there is war, my church, my school, my family, people who are sick, myself. Have the children put these cards into their prayer pockets; then tell them that each day they can pull a card from their pockets and pray for whatever is written on the card. If you like, help the children to make hangers for their pockets using yarn and a hole punch.

For younger children: Help the children assemble their prayer pockets; or prepare them in advance, if you wish. Before the session, gather stickers, make drawings, or cut pictures out of magazines to represent the following: a family, a church, a school, someone who is sick, a pet. Remember, you will need a set of stickers or pictures for each child. Let the children help attach the stickers or glue the pictures to index cards. Give a "set" of cards to each child and tell the children to put the cards in their prayer pockets. Then tell them that each day they can pull a card from their pockets and pray for whatever is pictured on the card.

Activity Two: Discovery Center (5-8 minutes)

For Older Children: Prepare ahead of time a cassette tape with readings of several favorite psalms of praise and prayer, such as Psalms 8, 23, 24, 46, 91, 96, 100, and 150. (If you have a Contemporary English Version of the Bible, read these psalms from this version.) Instruct the children to sit quietly and listen to one or more psalms. Explain that psalms were first used as the prayers and hymns of the Israelites, and today they continue to be used by the Christian church as prayers and hymns.

For All Children: Play one of the readings of the psalms from the cassette. Tell the children that the ancient Israelites used the psalms to pray to God and to offer God praise. Ask the children to listen again to the psalm and to come up with appropriate body motions and/or facial expressions for different parts of the psalm. Play the psalm one more time as the children accompany the reading with their body motions and facial expressions.

Activity Three: Study Center (10 minutes)

Distribute Bibles. Ask an older child to read Matthew 6:9-13 and 1 Thessalonians 5:16-18. Tell the children that the Scripture reading from Matthew reminds us that Jesus taught his disciples how to pray, and we, too, learn to pray as we learn the Lord's Prayer. First Thessalonians is a reminder that we are to give thanks to God.

Tell the children that just as they have been learning the Lord's Prayer and praying with their families during FaithHome, they are to continue to make prayer an important part of their everyday lives. Have them make prayer streamers to remind them of things they can pray for each and every day.

Prayer Streamers

For Older Children: Provide wide lengths of ribbon in assorted colors, fabric paint or markers, glue, and clothes hangers. Instruct each child to use fabric paint or markers to write a different prayer concern on as many pieces of ribbon as he or she wishes. Then have each child glue the ribbons to a clothes hanger. Tell the children they can hang their prayer streamers in their rooms as a reminder of what they can pray about each day.

For Younger Children: Have an older child or adult help each younger child make prayer streamers, writing the child's prayer concerns on the ribbons for him or her. Let the children decorate their streamers using markers or fabric paint before helping them attach the streamers to clothes hangers.

Closing Circle (5-10 minutes)

Call all the children together in a circle. Let each child share one thing he or she has learned or done. Ask each child to share one of the prayer concerns on his or her prayer streamers. Then pray the Lord's Prayer together. (Younger children may repeat lines or phrases after you.)

Using the poster on page 24, lead the children in signing the Apostles' Creed. Concentrate on the motions while you say the words. By now almost all the children should know it!

Listen to "Blessings Abound" and "Prayer Song," and then sing along with the FaithHome tape; or sing other favorites the children have enjoyed during the FaithHome experience. End with a spoken prayer of thanks for this learning time together.

Closing Time (15 minutes)

(1) As the children and adults come together, ask the adults to go with their children back to the tables where they worked on their praying hands. Invite each family to show their praying hands to the group and share one of their family's prayer concerns. After each family shares, lead the group in saying together, "We give thanks, O God, for this family (use their name[s]) and for their time with us."

(2) After every family has had a chance to speak, ask the group to enter with you into a time of prayer. Light the Christ candle, and ask one member of each family to bring their Christ candle and light it from the group's Christ candle; then dim the lights. Pray, asking for God's guidance for each family present and for strength to continue the commitment of study, discussion, reflection, and service as this group is ending and they continue the FaithHome experience on their own. (After the prayer, turn the lights back on.)

(3) Say together the Apostles' Creed, letting the children help lead the group in the motions they have learned.

(4) End with "Prayer Song," singing along with the FaithHome tape.

(5) Thank everyone for their participation in FaithHome and send them forth with a special blessing. Remind each family to take their family banner home with them as a special keepsake from their FaithHome experience.

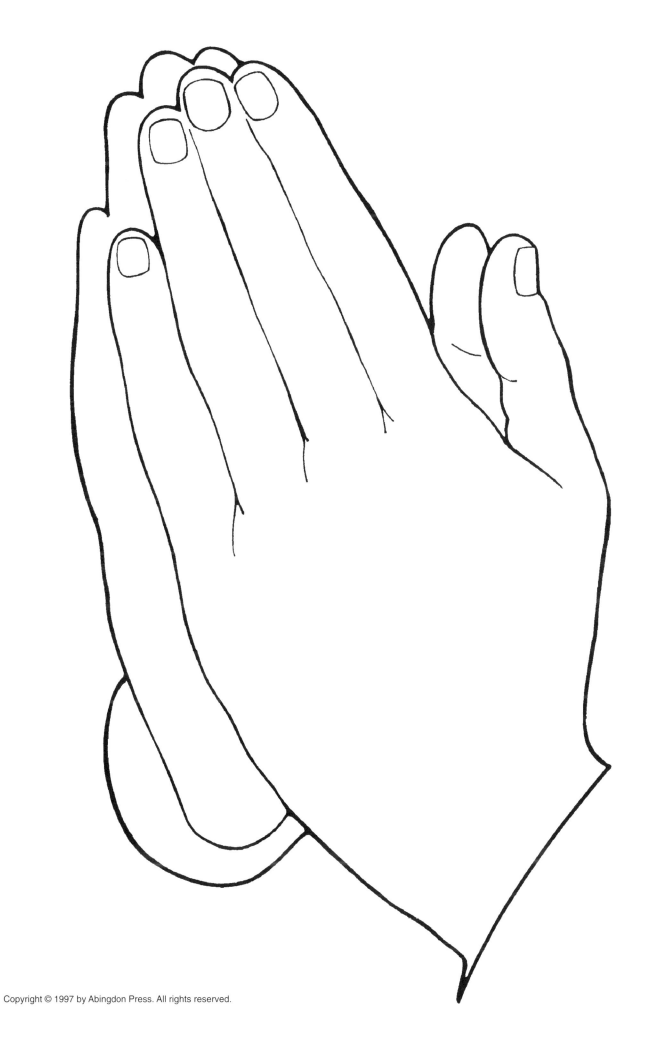

OPTIONAL RETREAT

One effective way to end the FaithHome experience is with an overnight retreat. This would be an optional event for the leaders and participants of your group. The first step is to appoint a "retreat director" who is to be responsible for planning the retreat. (The retreat director may be you or another leader or participant from your FaithHome group.) Planning tips for the retreat director; a suggested retreat schedule; and a planning guide for the retreat, which includes a list of the needed equipment and materials, are provided for you. Feel free to adapt or revise these materials as necessary for your particular group.

PLANNING TIPS FOR THE RETREAT LEADER

Appoint a "retreat director" who is responsible for planning the retreat. The retreat director should

—contract for a camp or retreat facility for overnight lodging and determine the fee needed from each family;

—make sure all those who have led the adult sessions and the children's sessions will be able to lead those respective sessions at the retreat;

—recruit additional persons to help with the retreat, including those who have worked in the nursery during your weekly FaithHome gatherings as well as others who can assist with the older children;

—plan for meals, or contract with the retreat center for meals;

—using the supply list provided, assemble the necessary supplies for all sessions;

—solicit congregational prayers for those who will be on retreat;

—arrange for a pastor to conduct Communion for closing worship;

—notify all participating families of the supplies they will need to bring for the retreat;

—prior to the retreat, send to all participating families the following note:

Dear _____:

I am so glad that your family is planning to be part of our FaithHome retreat. Enclosed is a list of items you will need to bring with you. You also will need the following items for our sessions together:

> *Bibles (for adults and for children)*
> *your FaithHome Family Guide*
> *your family's Christ candle*
> *recreational games or items your family enjoys*

If you have any questions, please do not hesitate to call.

> *Sincerely,*
>
> *(Name)*
> *Retreat Director*

THE RETREAT SCHEDULE

DAY 1

4:00 P.M.–7:00 P.M.
Arrival at retreat site

7:00 P.M.–8:30 P.M.
Session 1: Parents and children together

8:30 P.M.–10:00 P.M.
Fellowship, games, snacks

Day 2

9:00 P.M–12:00 NOON   Session 2

9:00 A.M.–9:45 A.M.
Parents and children together

9:45 A.M.–10:30 A.M
Separate sessions with parents and children

10:30 A.M.–10:45 A.M.
Break

10:45 A.M.–11:45 A.M.
Parents and children together

1:30 P.M.–3:30 P.M.   Session 3

1:30 P.M.–2:30 P.M.
Separate sessions with parents and children

2:30 P.M.–2:45 P.M.
Break

2:45 P.M.–3:30 P.M.
Closing worship

SESSION 1 - What We've Learned

 Materials Needed:

posterboard (one for each family), markers, glue, scissors, magazines and/or old church school curriculum, hymnals or copies of the Apostles' Creed (page 25) and other creeds of faith, newsprint (one sheet for each family), Christ candle for each family, matches, cassette tape player and FaithHome cassette tape, extra Bibles (for those who may have forgotten to bring their own)

7:00 P.M.–8:30 P.M.

In advance, set up tables or areas on the floor for each family. Place at each spot the following items: posterboard, markers, glue, scissors, newsprint, magazines and/or old church school curriculum, Christ candle.

(1) Invite each family to find a table or area where they can sit together; then say to the group:

Tonight we are going to reflect on the nine weekly gatherings we've had together. We also will talk about the things you have done together at home during the FaithHome experience. Before you are supplies for making a collage. Using pictures, words, and phrases, make a posterboard collage to tell about the experiences you have had as you have been learning and growing together in faith. (15-20 minutes)

(2) Remind the group that we have been thinking and talking together about what we believe. Ask if anyone can remember and recite the Apostles' Creed; have this person or persons lead the group in reciting it together. Ask if there are others who know additional creeds that they can recite for the group. (5 minutes)

(3) Ask each family to look for the sheet of newsprint on their table or in their area. Instruct each family to write on the newsprint three things they know they believe. Explain:

I'm sure you can think of many more than three things, but this is enough for the group litany we're going to compose in a few minutes. (10 minutes)

(4) Have the families come together in a circle. Ask each family to bring their collage, their sheet of

newsprint, and their Christ candle with them. Then have each family stand and tell about their collage. Encourage the group to clap for each family as they finish sharing. (15 minutes)

(5) Place all the Christ candles on one table. Ask a member from each family to come forward one at a time to light a Christ candle. As this person lights the candle, have the entire family stand and recite the beliefs or affirmations they have written on newsprint. Lead the entire group in saying "Amen" after each family's statement of belief. (5 minutes)

(6) Lead the group in singing songs from the FaithHome cassette tape as well as other songs they have enjoyed singing during the FaithHome experience. (10-15 minutes)

(7) Ask each family to name one story from the Bible or one Bible verse they have enjoyed studying during FaithHome. Read or recite these together. (15 minutes)

(8) Pray together, thanking God for this time of fellowship and learning together. (5 minutes)

SESSION 2 - Questions We Still Have

 Materials Needed:

For Full Group: FaithHome video, video player and monitor

For Adults: note cards, pencils, Bibles

For Children: shoe box, white paper for wrapping the shoe box, tape or glue, scissors, crayons and markers, note cards, construction paper

9:00 A.M.–9:45 A.M.

(1) Begin by sharing joys and concerns. Make a note of these as they are mentioned. Ask the group for specific prayer concerns they would like to raise. Note these also. Lead the group in prayer, including the joys and concerns mentioned by the group. (5 minutes)

(2) Say to the group:

We began each of our weekly FaithHome gatherings by viewing a video segment. These segments have helped us

focus our thoughts each week. Today I'm going to show all the segments consecutively. As you watch, think about questions you may have that you would like us to try to answer together during this retreat. Remember that no question is unimportant or silly. (40 minutes)

(3) After viewing the video, tell the adults where they will be meeting and let those who are working with the children lead them to their meeting space.

9:45 A.M.–10:30 A.M.

Adult Session

(1) Give each adult one or more note cards and ask the adults to write questions they still may have about God, the Christian faith, the church, or other topics that have arisen during the FaithHome experience. Allow a few minutes for each person to reflect privately on his or her questions. After time is up, collect all the note cards and set them aside. (10 minutes)

(2) Ask each person to get a Bible and turn with you to the Book of James. Divide the adults into four groups and assign each group a section of Scripture:

> Group 1: James 1:19-27
> Group 2: James 2:14-26
> Group 3: James 3:13-18
> Group 4: James 5:13-20

Instruct each group to discuss the following questions:

—What do you think James was trying to say in this passage?
—What message does this passage have for us today?
—How can I show faith within my family both by words and by actions? (15 minutes)

(3) Ask each group to summarize their Scripture passage and their findings regarding the passage. Allow 20 minutes for this activity. Then explain:

When we read and study the Scriptures, we must remember that **all** *our questions about a particular passage cannot be answered. We have read today from the Book of James because it helps us to know that our actions are important. As parents, what we do makes as strong or stronger a statement to our children as our words.*

Assure participants that you will address their questions after lunch during the afternoon session. (20 minutes)

Children's Session

Note: *This session can be set up in three different learning centers as you have done each week during FaithHome. After an opening circle activity, children can rotate through the centers in small groups before coming together for the closing circle. When the children enter the room or area, point out the activity in each center and explain what they are to do.*

OR

Depending upon the number and ages of children in your group and the number of "helpers" you have, you may do each of these activities sequentially between the two circle times.

Opening Circle (5 minutes)

Play a name game. Go around the circle and use the name of each person in a rhyme following this pattern:

> **This is Grace.**
> **She goes to a car race.**
> **She likes to eat licorice lace.**

Let the children come up with a silly place to go that rhymes with the child's name and a silly food to eat that rhymes with the name. If you have time, go around once again and see who can remember the place and food for each child.
  Show the children the activities they will be doing.

Activity One: Group Discussion (5-10 minutes)

Talk for a moment about the FaithHome video you watched just a few minutes ago. What did the children think about the youngsters in the video and what they had to say? What other questions would the children in your group have asked if they were making the video? Ask each child to tell one question he or she would like to ask his or her parents (or caregivers) about God, Jesus, the Bible, the church, or the Christian faith.

Activity Two: Art Center (15 minutes)

Question Box

Provide a shoe box, white paper, glue or tape, scissors, markers, and note cards. Let the children take turns helping to cover the box with white paper, wrapping the top of the box separately (so that the top may be lifted off). Have an older child or adult cut a slit in the top of the box. Let the children work together to decorate the box using markers.

Instruct each child to write on a note card the one question he or she would like to ask his or her parents (or caregivers). An older child or adult can help the younger children. Show them how to place the cards in the box.

Activity Three: Bible Study (10 minutes)

Help the children find Hebrews 13:1-3 in their Bibles; ask an older child to read the passage aloud. Give each child a piece of construction paper or drawing paper and ask him or her to draw a picture illustrating this Bible verse.

Closing Time: (5 minutes)

Call the children together in a circle. Place the question boxes in the center of the circle. Tell the children that they will be joining their parents in just a few minutes. At that time, you will read the questions from the question boxes and ask the parents to try to answer them. Tell the children that any parent can help answer a question; in other words, their own parents may not answer the question, but another adult in the room might.

10:30 A.M.–10:45 A.M.

Allow a short break for the children and adults.

10:45 A.M.–11:45 A.M.

Combined Session

(1) During this session, the adults will try to answer the questions the children have placed in the question box. If you can arrange the room in this way, ask the adults to sit in a circle in the middle of the room, with the children sitting around the outside of the circle.

(2) The leader of the children will draw one question at a time from the box and read it aloud. Then the leader will invite the adults to try to answer the question. Be sure to explain that any adult may answer any question.

(3) At the end of the time, ask the children and adults to stand and join hands and say or sing a blessing for the noon meal. Tell the group that the next session will be at 1:30 P.M., and they will meet in their separate groups at that time.

SESSION 3 - Next Steps

 Materials Needed:

For Adults: question box (see Session 2), note cards, pencils, newsprint, markers

For Children: strip of white cloth (6" x 4'), square of white cloth (4' x 4'), posterboard, markers, newsprint, paper plates, clay or play dough, candles to be used in worship

1:30 P.M.–2:30 P.M.

Adult Session

(1) Talk briefly about the morning session and the questions the children asked. Ask the adults what other questions have been asked in conversations at home during the FaithHome experience. Invite them to write these questions on note cards and place them in the question box. Go through the questions one at a time, encouraging the adults to help one another think about how to respond. (15 minutes)

(2) Tell the adults that the habits they have begun in FaithHome are meant to be continued. Ask each adult or couple prayerfully to consider what they can commit to do over the next year to continue the FaithHome experience in their home. Ask them also to think about what they need from the rest of the group or the congregation in order to make or keep that commitment. (10 minutes)

(3) Ask each adult or couple to share the commitment they are willing to make. List these commitments on newsprint. On a separate sheet of newsprint, list those things they need from the group or the congregation in order to make or keep this commitment. Plan together how to secure the support needed for all the families to live out their commitments. (30 minutes)

(4) Close with a prayer of thanks for the commitments listed. (5 minutes)

Children's Session

Note: *Rather than rotating through three activity centers, the children will work in three groups to make items to be used during the closing worship.*

Opening Circle (15 minutes)

Tell the children:

During the next hour, we are going to prepare some things that will be used in our time of worship together. When we come back together with the adults, we will have a closing service of Communion. We will be giving thanks for what we have learned together during FaithHome.

Lead the children in creating a brief litany that can be used in the worship service. Use this stem: "We thank you God for FaithHome because . . ." Let the children name things they are thankful for related to FaithHome; list these things on newsprint.
Tell the children that some of them will be using this list to create a poster to be used during worship. Some of them will be preparing a stole for the pastor to wear while serving Communion. Some will be preparing an altar cloth to be used for Communion. Others will be decorating plates for the Communion bread. Still others will be making candle holders for the candles.
Divide the children into small groups and explain to each group what they will be doing to help prepare for the closing worship.

Activity Groups: (30 minutes)

Group 1: Have this group make a stole for the pastor. The children will need a long strip of white cloth 6" x 4') and markers. Instruct them to write or draw on the cloth words or pictures of things they have learned during FaithHome.

Group 2: Have this group make a worship cloth. The children will need a square of white cloth (4' x 4') and markers. Instruct them to write or draw on the cloth words or pictures of things they have learned during FaithHome.

Group 3: Have this group make candle holders, plates for the Communion bread, and a poster of the litany. The children will need posterboard, markers, and the list made by the group during the opening circle. This group needs to include older children who are good at writing clearly. Ask the children to write the litany on the posterboard using letters that are large enough for everyone to read. Others in this group can use markers to decorate paper plates for the Communion bread and can make candle holders using clay or play dough.

Closing Time: (5 minutes)

Call the children back together in a circle. Ask them to bring those things that they have made for worship. Say a prayer of thanks for those things that they have made. As a group, go to where worship will be held and place the items for worship in that area.

2:30 P.M.–2:45 P.M.

Allow a short break for the children and adults.

2:45 P.M.–3:30 P.M.

For a time of closing worship, have a pastor lead the group in a Communion service, using the children's litany of thanks during the service. Be sure to use the other items created by the children during the service. End the service with prayer and a special blessing for each family.

APPENDIX 1:
Music

We Are Faith Families

We are faith fam - i - lies, ___ grow-ing in faith to - geth - er! We are faith fam - i - lies ___ serv - ing ___ the Lord!

1. Each one of us is God's child, ___ made in love and saved by grace. Broth - er and sis - ter of Je - sus, friend of the whole hu - man race.

2. The Bi - ble is our teach - er. The church pro-claims God's lov - ing call. Come ___ now, Ho - ly Spir - it, lead us to choose the good for us all.

We are

Fine

D.S. al Fine

WORDS: Dan Solomon
MUSIC: Joy Solomon
ARRANGEMENT: Linda Ray Miller

We Are the Church

Chorus

WORDS	MOTIONS
I am the church	*Point to self*
You are the church	*Point to someone in the group*
We are the church together	*Shake hands with someone*
All who follow Jesus	*Point up*
All around the world	*Make arms into a circle*
Yes we're the church together	*Join hands in a circle*

Verse 1

WORDS	MOTIONS
The church is not a building	*Draw a square in the air with hands*
The church is not a steeple	*Place hands together in a point*
The church is not a resting place	*Rest folded hands on one side of face*
The church is the people	*Point to another person*

Verse 2

WORDS	MOTIONS
We're many kinds of people	*Point around the circle*
With many kinds of faces	*Point to your face*
All colors and all ages, too, from	*Use hand to show height from small to tall*
All times and places	*Stretch out hand and make sweeping motion*

Verse 3

WORDS	MOTIONS
And when the people gather	*Stretch hands in front to form a circle*
There's singing and there's praying	*Fold hands in prayer*
There's laughing and there's crying sometimes	*Trace fingers from eyes down cheeks*
All of it saying	*Cup hands in megaphone fashion at mouth*

We Are the Church

WORDS: Richard K. Avery and Donald S. Marsh
MUSIC: Richard K. Avery and Donald S. Marsh

APPENDIX 2:
Bibliography
of
Recommended Resources

Family Ministry

Bernstein, Karen Jones, ed. *Church and Family Together: A Congregational Manual for Black Family Ministry.* Valley Forge: Judson Press, 1996.

This book is a good step-by-step guide for African American congregations. It includes basic information about the status of black families, along with congregational celebration and study suggestions and worship aids.

Fishburn, Janet F. *Parenting Is for Everyone: Living Out Our Baptismal Covenant.* Louisville, Kentucky: Presbyterian Mariner Publication, 1996.

This study for adults was written for Presbyterian congregations but also can be used in other denominations. It explores meanings and duties of families, along with looking at the church as "first family."

Olson, Richard P. and Joe H. Leonard, Jr. *A New Day for Family Ministry.* Bethesda, Maryland: The Alban Institute, 1996.

This book is excellent for those wishing to guide family ministry in a congregation. It includes a look at today's families with both their problems and their blessings and is especially effective in discussing what is needed in ministry.

Individual or Group Study

Fuchs, Nancy. *Our Share of Night, Our Share of Morning: Parenting as a Spiritual Journey.* San Francisco: HarperSanFrancisco, 1996.

This book discusses parenting as sacred space. Recommended for individuals or groups interested in more in-depth study.

It Takes More Than Love. Nashville: Ecu Film, 1996.

Based on the Search Institute Study of over 300,000 youth, this four-part video/print curriculum is designed to help parents and faith communities support the positive development of children. A student book, "What Kids Need to Know to Succeed," accompanies the video. (Contact Ecu Film, 810 Twelfth Ave., South, Nashville, TN 37203; 1-800-251-4091.)

Thompson, Marjorie. *Family, the Forming Center, Revised Edition.* Nashville: Upper Room Books, 1997.

This is one of the best books stating the case for family as a center for faith. It can be used as a study book by individuals or small groups.

Prayer/Spiritual Life

Cloyd, Betty Shannon. *Children and Prayer.* Nashville: Upper Room Books, 1997.

This comprehensive guide about how children relate to God provides concepts for teaching children about prayer and includes prayers written by children, prayers parents and caregivers can pray with children, interviews with children, and resources for further study.

Foster, Richard J. *Prayer: Finding the Heart's True Home.* San Francisco: HarperSanFrancisco, 1992.

This sensitive primer on prayer clarifies the prayer process, answers common misconceptions, and shows the way into prayers of contemplation, healing, blessing, forgiveness, and rest. It demonstrates how prayer can move us inward into personal transformation, upward toward intimacy with God, and outward to minister to others.

God's Little Devotional Book on Prayer. Tulsa: Honor Books, 1997.

This devotional companion presents the essential principles of developing a profound prayer experience. Each day's uplifting reading is accompanied by inspiring Scriptures and the wisdom of men and women who share their keys for effective prayer.

Herring, Annie. *Glimpses: Seeing God in Everyday Life.* Minneapolis: Bethany House, 1996.

Herring presents her own simple, honest encounters with God and relates insights that will inspire readers to see with new eyes the ordinary events of their lives and to recognize the handprint of God on each of their days.

Killinger, John. *Beginning Prayer.* Nashville: Upper Room Books, 1993.

Families who are beginning to pray for and with each other will find this to be a helpful resource. Several specific methods of prayer are included.

Nappa, Mike and Amy. *52 Fun Family Prayer Adventures.* Minneapolis: Augsburg Fortress, 1996.

These fresh prayer activities, which can be used in any family setting, are accompanied by Bible verses and prayer insights and quotes. A Scripture index also is included.

Wooden, Keith. *Teaching Children to Pray.* Grand Rapids: Zondervan, 1992.

Written in a practical and anecdotal style, this book helps parents and others teach children how to talk with God in a natural and intimate way.

Family Devotions

Evans, James L. *Bringing God Home: Family Devotions for the Christian Year.* Macon, Georgia: Smyth & Helwys Publishing, Inc., 1995.

This book follows the Christian year with suggested devotions for Monday through Thursday of each week. It includes activities, Scriptures, space for journaling, and ideas for mission and service.

Family Walk Devotional Bible. Grand Rapids: Zondervan, 1996.

This devotional Bible, which uses the New International Version, includes 260 devotions for Mondays through Fridays and 52 fun-filled weekend activities to make the Bible lessons come alive in creative ways designed to strengthen family bonds.

Jahsmann, Alan Hart and Martin P. Simon. *Little Visits for Families*. St. Louis, Missouri: Concordia Publishing House, 1961, 1995.

Created for families (with children ages 7-10) to read together, these "little visits" include Scripture, meditations based on daily life, prompts for talking together as a family, additional Bible readings, and family prayers.

Johnson, Greg. *What Would You Do If . . . ?* Ann Arbor, Michigan: Servant Publications, 1995.

Designed to be used with children ages six to twelve, this book contains read-aloud devotions to help strengthen Christian values. Includes discussion questions for families to use.

Loth, Paul J. *God Takes Care of Me*. Nashville: Thomas Nelson, 1995.

This book provides 75 devotions for families with young children.

Nappa, Mike and Amy. 52 *Fun Family Devotions*. Minneapolis: Augsburg Fortress, 1994.

This book provides a year's worth of devotions that the entire family will enjoy.

The One-Year Book of Family Devotions, Vols. 1 & 2. Wheaton, Illinois: Tyndale House, 1988 & 1989.

Each volume provides an entire year's worth of devotions for the entire family to share.

Books, Bibles, and Devotions for Children

Abraham, Angela and Ken. *Praise and Worship: A Devotional for Little Ones*. Dallas: Word Publishing, Inc., 1996.

This children's devotional, based on the International Children's Bible, includes songs, Bible stories, poems, activities, and prayers that teach children how to praise God.

Batchelor, Mary. *My Own Book of Prayers*. Nashville: Abingdon Press, 1996.

This collection of more than 100 prayers, designed to appeal to children ages 5-8, focuses on the child's own world and experience. The prayers are arranged by theme and include familiar favorites as well as fresh contemporary prayers.

Beers, V. Gilbert. *The Early Reader's Bible*. Sisters, Oregon: Gold and Honey Books, 1991.

This colorfully illustrated Bible is designed for beginning readers and includes 64 easy-to-read Bible stories, stimulating questions, and real-life applications to increase children's understanding of God's Word.

The Children's Daily Devotional Bible. Nashville: Thomas Nelson, 1996.

This child-friendly devotional Bible uses the Contemporary English Version and is targeted to ages 6-11.

Everyday Prayers for Children. Nashville: Dimensions for Living, 1993.

This pocket-sized collection of prayers is designed to be shared with children of all ages.

Every Day with God. Dallas: Word Publishing, Inc., 1990.

Based on the International Children's Bible, this devotional for ages 7-10 features five short Bible readings each week that take children from Creation to Revelation in one year.

Jahsmann, Alan Hart and Martin P. Simon. *Little Visits with God*. St. Louis: Concordia Publishing House, 1957, 1995.

These devotions for children ages 7-10 are designed to nurture faith as they encourage children to learn about God. Each devotion includes a Bible verse, a life-related meditation, questions to help children get involved, suggested Scripture readings for older kids, and a prayer related to the day's theme.

Kids' Devotional Bible. Grand Rapids: Zondervan, 1996.

This children's Bible uses the New International Reader's Version and includes five weekday devotions and one weekend devotion.

Lindvall, Ella K. *Read-Aloud Bible Stories, Vol. 1-4*. Chicago: Moody Press, 1982-1995.

This four-volume series presents favorite Bible stories in a read-aloud format with accompanying illustrations.

Lucas, Daryl J., ed. *God Is Great*. Wheaton, Illinois: Tyndale House, 1995.

This book is perfect for active, read-to-me children or early readers. It includes Bible passages for every day, questions to talk about, and a prayer for parents and children to say together.

O'Neal, Debbie Trafton. *I Can Pray with Jesus: The Lord's Prayer for Children*. Minneapolis: Augsburg Fortress, 1997.

In familiar words and colorful pictures common to a

young child's experience, this book brings to life each part of the Lord's Prayer and assures children of God's love for them. Action prayers, fingerplays, and songs are also included.

O'Neal, Debbie Trafton. *Thank You for This Food: Action Prayers, Songs, and Blessings for Mealtime*. Minneapolis: Augsburg Fortress, 1997.

This delightfully refreshing collection of action prayers, songs, and table graces includes both traditional and contemporary prayers to make giving thanks at mealtimes a joyful experience for the whole family. Full-color illustrations throughout.

Rich, Scharlotte. *I Love My Mommy*. Sisters, Oregon: Questar, 1995.

This beautifully illustrated book shows ethnically diverse families engaged in a variety of family activities while they talk about life, God, and love.

Rock, Lois. *The Lord's Prayer for Children*. Batavia, Illinois: Lion Publishing, 1993.

This beautifully illustrated children's book includes the text of the Lord's Prayer along with familiar words and pictures that bring the meaning to life for young children.

Simon, Mary Manz. *Little Visits Every Day*. St. Louis: Concordia Publishing House, 1988, 1995.

These devotions intended for parents or other adults to share with children (ages 4-7) use familiar things to show God at work in the world. Each devotion includes a Bible verse, a life-related meditation, ways to help children get involved, and a prayer starter or suggestion.

Christian Parenting

Carmichael, Bill. *Seven Habits of a Healthy Home*. Grand Rapids: Tyndale House, 1997.

This book discusses how to cultivate seven "habits" or characteristics necessary for a home where children can grow in godly virtues and character.

Frydenger, Tom and Adrienne. *The Blended Family*. Grand Rapids: Chosen Books, 1984.

This book helps parents of blended families break free from the guilt of past marital failure, deal with problems of "extended families" left from previous marriages, overcome sibling rivalries, and build new family traditions.

Krueger, Caryl. *Single with Children*. Nashville: Abingdon Press, 1993.

This "survival manual" for single parents includes 144 ideas for coping and getting it all done.

Richmond, Gary. *Successful Single Parenting: Going It Alone*. Eugene, Oregon: Harvest House, 1990.

This book suggests how single parents can raise healthy, confident children in today's complex world.

Stephens, Larry D. *Your Child's Faith*. Grand Rapids: Zondervan, 1996.

This book shows parents and other caregivers how to build a foundation for their children's faith. It explores the different stages of a growing, vital faith, from infancy to adulthood.

Westerhoff, John H. III. *Bringing Up Children in the Christian Faith*. San Francisco: HarperSanFrancisco, 1984.

This book is an excellent, in-depth resource for all Christian parents.

Family Fun and Activities

Erickson, Donna. *Prime Time Together with Kids: Creative Ideas, Activities, Games, and Projects*. Minneapolis: Augsburg Fortress, 1989.

These fun ideas for families are perfect for "prime time" or anytime.

Krueger, Caryl Waller. *365 Ways to Love Your Child*. Nashville: Abingdon Press, 1995.

Whether a child is preschool, elementary, or teen age, this book will help parents and others find just the right way to show love through words and actions and instill within a child a sense of security and of being loved.

Merrill, Dean and Grace. *Together at Home*. Wheaton, Illinois: Tyndale House, 1985, 1996.

This book is full of simple and creative ideas to help parents and other caregivers raise a godly family and have fun in the process. Included are more than 100 ideas for a weekly family night.

Rogovin, Anne. *Turn Off the TV and . . .* Nashville: Abingdon Press, 1995.

Rogovin presents a treasury of activities that families can do as alternatives to watching television.

Family Outreach

Appling, Mary Ann Ward. *Making Memories: Ideas for Family Missions Involvement*. Birmingham: New Hope Publishers, 1993.

This book is a compilation of ideas, appropriate for varying ages and settings, for involving families in missions.

Garborg, Rolf. *The Family Blessing*. Dallas: Word Publishing, 1990.

This is the account of one family's experience of

giving and receiving blessings in the ordinary times of life. Whether or not you use the suggestions provided in the book, the concept is worthy to pursue. Hints for families are included.

Periodicals

Pockets Magazine. Nashville: The Upper Room.

A magazine, written for children ages six to twelve, that includes stories, prayers, games, and a daily Scripture guide so that children can study the Bible on their own. Published 11 times annually.

DevoZine. Nashville: The Upper Room.

A magazine for youth that includes daily meditations, Scriptures, and suggestions for living. Published bimonthly.

Alive Now. Nashville: The Upper Room.

A magazine that is written to strengthen the faith life of groups and individuals and that could be especially appropriate for families with older teens or young adults. Published bimonthly.

ENDNOTES

WEEK 1

1. Trevor Huddleston, *I Believe: Reflections on the Creed* (London: Fount Paperbacks, 1986), 13.

2. Ted Jennings, *Loyalty to God* (Nashville: Abingdon, 1992).

3. Eduard Schweizer, Class handout, Princeton Theological Seminary, as cited in Elizabeth Rankin Geitz, *Gender and the Nicene Creed* (Harrisburg: Morehouse Publishing, 1995), 3.

WEEK 2

1. Tobias Clausnitzer, 1668; translated by Catherine Winkworth, 1863. *The United Methodist Hymnal* (Nashville: Copyright © 1989 The United Methodist Publishing House), 85.

2. Mechtild of Magdeburg, Germany, 13th century; *The United Methodist Hymnal* (Nashville: Copyright © 1989 The United Methodist Publishing House), 104.

3. J. Robert Wright, *Readings for the Daily Office From the Early Church* (New York: Church Hymnal Corporation, 1991), 132.

4. St. Cyril of Jerusalem, *The Catechetical Lectures of St. Cyril of Jerusalem* (Oxford: J. H. Parker, 1838), 152.

5. Tilden H. Edwards, *Spiritual Friend: Reclaiming the Gift of Spiritual Direction* (New York: Paulist Press, 1980), 138-39.

6. The Holy Bible: New Revised Standard Version study helps: "God: Creator and Redeemer" (Nashville: Thomas Nelson Publishers, for Cokesbury, 1990), 12.

WEEK 3

1. Karl Barth, *Credo* (London: Hodder and Stoughton, 1935), 45.

2. St. Athanasius, *On the Incarnation* (Crestwood, NY: St. Vladimir's Seminary Press, 1989), 29.

3. J. Robert Wright, *Readings for the Daily Office From the Early Church* (New York: The Church Hymnal Corp., 1991), 42.

4. Elizabeth Rankin Geitz, *Gender and the Nicene Creed* (Harrisburg, PA: Morehouse Publishing, Inc., 1995), 50.

5. Marjorie J. Thompson, *Family, the Forming Center* (Nashville: Upper Room Books, 1989), 24.

WEEK 4

1. The Nicene Creed, third article.

2. Prayer of Henry vanDyke, U.S.A., 20th century, alt. as found in *The United Methodist Hymnal* (Nashville: Copyright © 1992 The United Methodist Publishing House), 407.

3. Saint Basil, *On the Holy Spirit,* (Crestwood, N.Y.: St. Vladimir's Seminary Press, 1980), 46, 60, 73.

4. Elizabeth Rankin Geitz, *Gender and the Nicene Creed* (Harrisburg, PA: Morehouse Publishing, 1995), 77.

WEEK 5

1. Trevor Huddleston, *I Believe: Reflections on the Creed* (London: Fount Paperbacks, 1986), 72, as cited in *Gender and the Nicene Creed* by Elizabeth Rankin Geitz (Harrisburg, PA: Morehouse Publishing, 1995), 85.

2. "We Are the Church," by Richard K. Avery and Donald S. Marsh, 1972; found in *The United Methodist Hymnal* (Nashville: Copyright © 1989 The United Methodist Publishing House), 558.

3. Marjorie J. Thompson, *Family, the Forming Center* (Nashville: Upper Room Books, 1989), 20-21.

4. Delores Leckey, U.S. Bishops' Committee on the Laity, as cited by Marjorie J. Thompson, *Family, the Forming Center* (Nashville: Upper Room Books, 1989), 23.

WEEK 6

1. Nancy Fuchs, *Our Share of Night, Our Share of Morning: Parenting as a Spiritual Journey* (San Francisco: Harper San Francisco, 1996), 11.

WEEK 7

1. Marjorie J. Thompson, *Family, the Forming Center* (Nashville: Upper Room Books, 1989), 105.

2. Ibid.

WEEK 8

1. Marjorie J. Thompson, *Family, the Forming Center* (Nashville: Upper Room Books, 1989), 92-94.

2. Ibid, 91.

3. Ibid, 92.

WEEK 9

1. Nancy Fuchs, *Our Share of Night, Our Share of Morning: Parenting as a Spiritual Journey* (San Francisco: HarperSan Francisco, 1996), 111.

2. Ibid, 14.

3. Marjorie J. Thompson, *Family, the Forming Center* (Nashville: Upper Room books, 1989), 27. References are to *The Practice of the Presence of God,* a compilation of letters by, conversations with, and reminiscences about Brother Lawrence of the Resurrection in a new translation by Robert J. Edmonson, ed. Hal M. Helms (Orleans, Mass: Paraclete Press, 1985); and to Evelyn Underhill, *Practical Mysticism* (New York: E.P. Dutton, 1943).

4. Ibid, 57.

5. Ibid, 58.

6. Ibid, 67.